ACTIVITY-BASED COST MANAGEMENT

MAKING IT WORK

A Manager's Guide to Implementing and
Sustaining an Effective ABC System

ACTIVITY-BASED COST MANAGEMENT

MAKING IT WORK

A Manager's Guide to Implementing and Sustaining an Effective ABC System

GARY COKINS

McGraw-Hill

New York   San Francisco   Washington, D.C.   Auckland   Bogotá
Caracas   Lisbon   London   Madrid   Mexico City   Milan
Montreal   New Delhi   San Juan   Singapore
Sydney   Tokyo   Toronto

McGraw-Hill

A Division of The McGraw-Hill Companies

©The McGraw-Hill Companies, Inc., 1996

Library of Congress Cataloging–in–Publication Data

Cokins, Gary
    Activity-based cost management : making it work : a manager's guide
to implementing and sustaining an effective ABC system / Gary
Cokins.
        p.   cm.
    Includes index.
    ISBN 0–7863–0740–4
    1. Activity-based costing.   2. Managerial accounting.   3. Cost.
control.   I. Title.
HF5686.C8C657   1996
658.15′52—dc20   95–48434

Printed in the United States of America
    5 6 7 8 9 0 BS 3 2 1 0 9 8 7

DEDICATION

This book is dedicated to the late Robert A. Bonsack, a friend, a mentor, and a craftsman in the field of advanced cost management.

ACKNOWLEDGMENTS

*Effective adult learning results from real experience
and collaborative partnering with trusting teammates.
I'd like to thank the following friends for their
assistance and support in writing this book:*

Michael Andrud
Anik Bose
Herb Crowther
Joe Donnelly
Bill Hass
Steve Markevich
Joel Munch
Hugh Pinkus
Ron Plachy
Jack Shaw
Lew Soloway
Hal Thilmony
Pete Zampino
and my wife, Pam Tower

INTRODUCTION

Gradually, managerial accountants have become aware of the vanishing relevance of the numbers they produce for end-users and decision makers. In 1994, Professor John K. Shank of Dartmouth College said at the Institute of Management Accountants' 75th Anniversary Conference in New York City:

> Traditional accounting is at best useless, and at worst dysfunctional and misleading.

Those are pretty strong words. The audience was silent. But Shank continued to describe the imminent "sea change" that will occur in managerial accounting. He described how cost management will be to the 1990s what total quality management was to the 1980s.

Activity-based costing (ABC) is part of that sea change. ABC is not a replacement for the traditional general ledger accounting. Rather, it is a *translator* or *overlay,* as in Figure 1, that lies between the cost accumulators or the expenditure account balances in the general ledger and the end-users who apply cost data in decision making. ABC converts inert cost data into relevant information so that the users can take action.

ABC initially captured managements' attention in the early 1980s as a superior product and service costing technique. ABC removed the grotesquely distorting effect of broad-brushed overhead allocators, like labor hours or sales dollars. It replaced cost allocations with substantially more realistic cost assignments and consequently much greater accuracy. Then, in the 1990s, managers discovered that the same data they generated to recompute their ABC product or service costs could also be used to gain better insights and manage their product design and process design costs. It could also be used for performance measurements that align with business processes.

ABC is becoming increasingly more important for both identifying improvement opportunities and measuring the realized benefits of performance initiatives on an after-the-fact basis. Today's traditional costing practices show very little about the costs of cross-functional business processes and even less about where the non-value-added costs are. Further, when asked to detail their *actual* cost savings or cost avoidance realized from a project, managers cannot adequately do so.

Beyond thinking of ABC as a much better costing tool is recognizing it as truly an organizational methodology. Senior managers have been

FIGURE 1

ABC/ABM Reassigns Costs

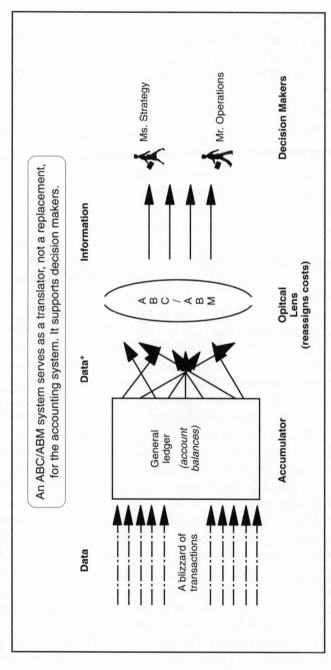

An ABC/ABM system serves as a translator, not a replacement, for the accounting system. It supports decision makers.

Data

A blizzard of transactions

Accumulator

General ledger
(account balances)

Data⁺

Opitcal Lens
(reassigns costs)

A
B
C
/
A
B
M

Information

Ms. Strategy

Mr. Operations

Decision Makers

frustrated by the difficulties in bringing about change within their organizations. Behavioral change management is receiving increasingly wider attention, and ABC data is playing an important role with it.

In short, only activity-based costing supports process-based thinking that leads to smarter decision making. This book expands on its predecessor, *An ABC Manager's Primer,* by going beyond describing just *what* it is. This book explains *why* to use ABC, *what* the calculus is supporting ABC, and *how* to implement ABC.

To repeat a warning from the first book, ABC simply produces data. Data provide means to ends. What matters are ends. However, there are lots of popular management improvement programs, including fads that trip over each other because they are so interconnected. ABC data help managers see the interconnectivity of time, quality, capacity, flexibility, and cost; activity-based management (ABM) allows them to navigate through the management fads and into the faster currents of high-payback performance improvement programs.

This book is intended to put the "management" back into management reporting. In many ways, ABC/ABM data are simple in means and rich in ends. Of course, the ends are decisions made with the data. This book is for those interested in fully exploiting cost data. Take the learning and move on to mastery.

I welcome all questions or comments at my e-mail address:

garyfarms@aol.com

Gary Cokins

ॐ

In God we trust. All others bring data!

Anonymous

CONTENTS

Chapter 8

Common Misconceptions about ABC/ABM   199

Chapter 9

Sustaining the ABC/ABM System   205

Chapter 10

Final Thoughts on ABC/ABM   215

LIST OF FIGURES

Chapter 3

Chapter 4

Chapter 5

Chapter 6

Chapter 7

CHAPTER 1

ABC/ABM

WHAT IT IS AND IS NOT

Today's management accounting information, driven by the procedures and cycle of the organization's financial reporting system, is too late, too aggregated, and too distorted to be relevant for managers' planning and control decisions.

H. Thomas Johnson and Robert S. Kaplan[1]

1–1. STATE OF THE UNION: THE ISSUES WITH ABC/ABM

The overarching issue with ABC/ABM involves its perception as just another way to spin financial data rather than its use as mission-critical managerial information. The Information Age we are entering can be mind-boggling. In our future, as technology advances, so will the demand to access massive amounts of relevant information. The companies and organizations that survive will be those that can answer these questions:

"How do we access all this data?"

"What do we do with it?"

"How do we shape the data and put it into a form with which we can work?"

"What will happen when we apply technologies developed *during* the Information Age *for* the Information Age?

Clearly, as information technology evolves, organizations will increase their effectiveness. Further, as markets change, companies and organizations will run into global competitors that increasingly look to information and information technology for competitive advantage. ABC/ABM is involved in this broad arena of "outsmartsmanship."

---

1. H. Thomas Johnson and Robert S. Kaplan, *Relevance Lost: The Rise and Fall of Management Accounting* (Boston, MA: Harvard Business School Press, 1987), p. 1.

What are today's burning issues with implementing ABC/ABM? The answers depend on the starting point of an organization. There appear to be three sequenced starting points: (1) one for beginners, (2) one for pilots, and (3) one for advanced, mature users (see Figure 1–1). Each starting point is unique and discussed below.

1. Since the late 1980s, the concepts of ABC/ABM have been sufficiently explained in seminars and published articles; by now most financial managers and many operations personnel adequately understand what ABC/ABM is. That is not the problem anymore for organizations wanting to begin implementation of ABC/ABM. The beginners' key issue today is *how to get started.* Their employees intuitively feel that their financial reporting both blocks the view of true costs across business processes as well as distorts product and service costs. In sum, employees have few reliable facts, severely inaccurate product and service costs, and little true cost visibility. Beginner organizations can't get started on ABC/ABM for a variety of reasons, including some users' fear of accountability as well as misconceptions that ABC/ABM involves a mud slide of data with horrendous updating and reporting problems. These and more reasons are discussed in Chapter 8.

2. The issues with the ABC/ABM pilot starting point involve *avoiding implementation failure.* Over these past few years, the jungle drums have been beating between other companies describing the lack of success with ABC/ABM, and consequently, newly formed project teams are cautious. Companies that have ventured into an ABC/ABM pilot are motivated to move away from their traditional cost system and the bad decisions it is causing; but they also appreciate that when they do change, there are preventions they can take to assure a successful implementation. Chapter 2 explains why ABC/ABM systems can fail and how to prevent that undesirable outcome.

3. The third starting point is that of the advanced, mature users. These companies usually have two or more pilots that have been in progress for well over a year. They are moving toward wide employee acceptance of this new form of financial data

FIGURE 1-1

Three Starting Points for ABC/ABM

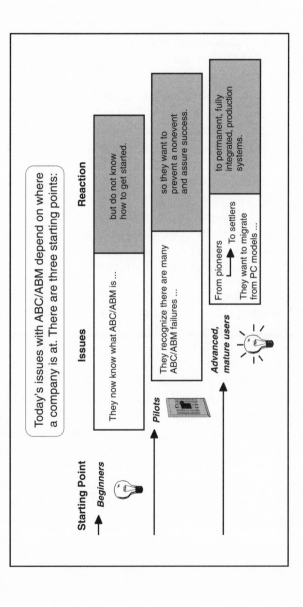

and increasing user demands for more frequent reporting, for selective greater detail, or for integration with other application software systems, like their customer order quotation systems, which are still harnessed to the old, flawed traditional cost data. The advanced users' key issue is how to migrate from their PC-based models that take periodic cost snapshots to a *permanent, fully-integrated production ABC/ABM system.*

This is no small task because the pilots were championed by strong "pioneer-types" of individuals who raced the clock to maintain momentum and left little documentation behind when implementing their pilot. A permanent ABC/ABM production system must be repeatable and reliable, and this involves technical information systems personnel and their end-users, who we can refer to as the "settlers." Settlers like predictability and consistency. Settlers often feel like they are left behind to clean up the mess the pioneers created before they moved on to other positions or companies. Chapter 9 further discusses system integration of ABC/ABM.

Regardless of a company's starting point with ABC/ABM, much more attention must be placed on stimulating the nonaccountants and end-users to buy into ABC/ABM concepts and data.

Jonathan B. Schiff, former editor of the Cost Management Group of the Institute of Management Accountants (IMA) monthly *Cost Management Update,* summarized ABC's take-off problem in the November 1993 issue. He described the acceptance of ABC/ABM as an imbalance between the supply and demand side of an equation. The substantial increase in ABC/ABM training and development programs, mainly directed to finance and accounting managers, represents a hefty supply side of the equation.

The demand side is the active stimulation of internal end-users to apply ABC/ABM information in their decisions and analyses. This has been weak. Figure 1–2 shows this imbalance. Without end-user interest on the demand side, the upgraded supplier will have difficulty integrating the new information into the end-users' decision-making habits. If there is not a healthy relationship between the accountants and their internal customers, then merely upgrading the supply side could have a negligible effect on improving the organization's decision-making capabilities.

FIGURE 1-2

Imbalance in Current ABC/ABM Acceptance

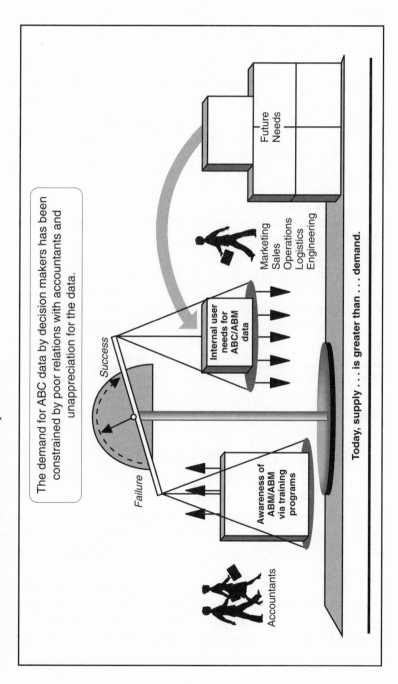

The demand for ABC data by decision makers has been constrained by poor relations with accountants and unappreciation for the data.

Success

Failure

Accountants

Awareness of ABM/ABM via training programs

Internal user needs for ABC/ABM data

Marketing
Sales
Operations
Logistics
Engineering

Future Needs

Today, supply . . . is greater than . . . demand.

End-users will assume no change, resulting in the same outputs as in the past—information that is late, difficult to understand, inaccurate, confusing, and overly complex.

The shame is it is only through the *application* of ABC/ABM technology, not the technology itself, that we get the full impact of any investment in better cost management techniques and information. One can only create value for customers by applying ABC/ABM.

Simply put, ABC/ABM has two groups operating too much in isolation from the other: The inventors (accountants or project team) and the end-users of the ABC/ABM technology. The end-users do not believe that the inventors understand their problem. And the inventors believe they are solving the end-users' problem. One possesses the need, while the other possesses the technology and know-how. This gap in communications, knowledge, and understanding must and will be closed through better collaboration.

In summary, there are no lack of issues for the ABC/ABM movement. The ABC/ABM method is certainly more correct than the traditional accounting system's; but there is so much more involved in creating wide acceptance and deploying its information. In my opinion, the biggest problem today with ABC/ABM is that while many companies have been occupied with the what and the how-to of the method, they have neglected the why. Why use a new kind of financial data? The next section provides the locations where ABC/ABM data can help an organization improve itself.

1–2. POPULAR BUSINESS IMPROVEMENT APPROACHES

Today organizations want business improvement programs that create value and ultimately bring profits to the bottom line. They want to convert carbon-based coal into diamonds. Companies appear less interested in improvement programs that are only value-enabling, and that only locate the carbon. They want value-creating programs.

Figure 1–3 lists five of the most popular business improvement approaches that many companies today are consciously or subconsciously applying. The diagram simply shows a corrective performance feedback loop that starts and ends with customers. It reveals that organizations try

FIGURE 1-3

Five Popular Approaches to Business Improvement

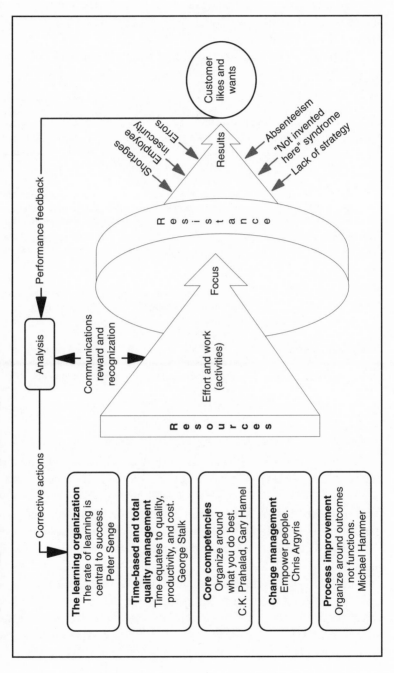

to focus their "4M" resources (manpower, machines, money, and materials) to produce desired results while constantly overcoming obstacles and organizational resistance.

The five popular business improvement methods are as follows:

Method	Premise	Thought Leader/Organization
The learning organization	We compete on knowledge, and the speed of organizational learning is critical.	Peter Senge, Massachusetts Institute of Technology
Time-based and total quality management	Nonconformance to achievable plans erodes performance.	George Stalk, Boston Consulting Group, and Dr. W. Edwards Deming
Core competencies	Deal from your market-critical strengths, and outsource your less critical weaknesses.	C. K. Prahalad, University of Michigan, and Gary Hamel, London Business School
Organizational behavior	People matter. Really matter. Resistance to change, incentives, and empowerment is not fluff.	Chris Argyris, Harvard Business School
Process improvement	Superior processes provide longer-sustaining competitive advantages than do products. Be innovative.	Michael Hammer, formerly Massachusetts Institute of Technology

Although ABC/ABM can serve as "initiative accelerators" to all five methods, its largest impact is on the last two. With regard to change management, ABC/ABM presents emotionally compelling facts that stimulate workers to want to change the way things are. With regard to process improvement, ABC/ABM quantifies the business process across the organization and highlights where the waste or opportunities are located.

One of the five methods described above combines total quality management (TQM) and cycle-time reduction (also referred to as just-in-time [JIT] or synchronous management). The prevailing logic with this form of improvement program has been that if you improve quality or reduce lead time, you effectively are removing waste, error, and low value-adding work content—and therefore costs will take care of themselves. That logic is now being challenged in some circles, but debating managerial philosophies can be like religious wars. Chapter 5 expands on some of the failed promises from TQM and JIT improvement programs. ABC/ABM can help make good on those promises.

A common employee complaint concerns the "program-of-the-month" approach, that is, following management fads with negligible long-term impact. Management's dilemma involves a trade-off: A company must do lots of good things simultaneously, but organizations also have a natural tendency to lose focus. Therefore, organizations need guidance and reinforcement of specific direction through periodic programs to emphasize something important; but, in the long run, everything is connected to everything. How can management prioritize what to work on? ABC/ABM can help.

Simply put, ABC/ABM is a tool, not a solution. It brings visibility of the symptoms of problems from which effective solutions can be inferred. In some cases, ABC/ABM brings visibility to that which has never been seen before; in other cases, it replaces existing flawed and highly misleading cost data caused by bad and distorting allocations. ABC/ABM has four objectives:

1. To eliminate or minimize low value-adding costs.
2. To introduce efficiency and effectiveness and thus streamline the value-adding activities that are executed in business processes to improve the yield.
3. To find the root causes of problems and correct them. Remember, costs are a symptom.
4. To remove distortions caused by poor assumptions and bad cost allocations.

Regardless of the performance improvement methods and tools that companies choose to apply, they should be aware that their enterprises are subject to certain natural properties, just like we are subject to physical laws of the universe such as gravity and the speed of light. One commonly overlooked natural property of business is that time, cost, and quality are linked, not independent of one another. All improvement efforts, continuous or breakthrough, are intended to increase value for one or more stakeholders. The goal is for efficient responsiveness with profit (refer to Figure 1–4).

Today's managers are recognizing how systemic and interconnected their work is. That is one reason team-based managing has become so

FIGURE 1-4

Interconnectivity of Time, Cost, and Quality

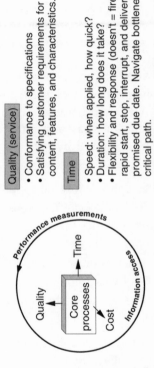

All improvement efforts, continous or breakthough, are intended to increase value for one or more stakeholders. The goal is for efficient responsiveness with profit.

Quality (service)
- Conformance to specifications
- Satisfying customer requirements for content, features, and characteristics.

Time
- Speed: when applied, how quick?
- Duration: how long does it take?
- Flexibility and response (doesn't = firefighting): rapid start, stop, interrupt, and deliver on promised due date. Navigate bottlenecks for critical path.

Stakeholders   Power
- Employees   Obliterate
- Management   Veto
- Customers   Coach
- Bankers   User
- Shareholders   Victim
- Pensioners
- Communities
- Regulators

Performance measurements

Quality

Core processes

Time

Cost

Information access

Cost (capacity)
- Fungible conversions of quality/time relationship
- Usually measures effect, not cause
- The enterprise engine's
  - Emission test (waste)
  - Fuel gauge (consumption)
  - Tachometer (acceleration)
  - Torque (agility)

popular. There are no more "island solutions." Businesses today must si-multaneously behave better, faster, and cheaper—quality, time, and cost. No more can companies pick two and let the third one slide. They have to consider the three elements all together. There must be integration.

As a consequence, there is a convergence of management disci-plines. A surprisingly large number of employees can pretty well under-stand the interconnectivity of how a business works as an integrated sys-tem. This is a new age.

What is the role of cost data in this systemic model? When you cut to the chase, costs are simply the residual of people or equipment doing activities. Costs are a derivative. They are a dependent variable—the re-sult of work being done and things being purchased. They reflect an im-pact. Costs are the shadow of a body or the echo of a sound. Costs are sometimes viewed as symptoms, representing deeper-rooted causes.

An analogy for an ABM cost model is an emission testing and diag-nostic instrument for automobiles—it captures the auto's exhaust for a short interval and then checks its fuel consumption rates (costs) and pu-rity content (value). The car engine's pistons, rods, carburetors, and in-jection mechanisms are combusting (the activities) gasoline (the re-sources), while the emission tester (the ABM model) gives feedback on rates and purity.

Section 1–3 below compresses an imaginary textbook on ABC/ABM into a few pages. By shortening the background on ABC/ABM, this book can focus on how to implement and use ABC/ABM.

1–3. THE EMERGING CONSENSUS ON ABC/ABM

ABC/ABM data are currently not being used as a managerial command-and-control tool. In fact, quite the opposite. The most popular uses of the new financial data involve *forward planning* and *predictive modeling* of the cost impact of decisions that will affect the future. Rarely is ABC/ABM data used with an "accounting police" mentality in a similar way that standard cost and budget variance data and analyses are fre-quently used to curb department spending and punish irresponsible spenders. ABC/ABM enhances the new image of financial accountants as *partners,* not enforcers and gatekeepers, with sales and operations per-sonnel in navigating and coordinating the various business improvement program options and initiatives. Figure 1–5 presents the emphasis on pre-dictive planning.

F I G U R E 1-5

From Data to Actions

The linkage between the ABC/ABM cost flow data and organizational decision making emphasizes a more forward-looking view than a historical one.

Examples:

- Order/customer quotes
- Spending/investment justification
- Return on quality (ROQ)
- Process-based requirement planning
- Target costing
- Activity-based budgeting

Command and control

Diagnostics / Assessment

Predictive planning

Yesterday   Today   21st Century

The role of the accountant as a partner is a theme throughout this book. In many ways, the role of cost accounting itself will likely drift back to where it was located earlier this century: in operations. A note of caution is that the job of the accountant may diminish as a result of automated transaction technologies, changing policy assumptions tolerating greater risk, knowledge about the true costs caused by controls, and finally the shift of the traditional cost accountant's job responsibilities to end-users who can analyze data and resolve errors and disputes themselves.

Returning to the subject of ABC/ABM, a computerized literature search on the topic would generate a fairly thick pile of pages. This section summarizes the current thoughts about the ABC/ABM movement. It starts with discussing the thinking behind computing the costs of processes and then computing the costs of products and services. Then target costing will be touched on. This section finishes with recent thoughts on the accounting practice of full absorption of so-called fixed costs, the grueling annual budget exercise, and the future of standard cost accounting practices. The remainder of this book addresses designing, implementing, and using ABC/ABM systems.

1–3A. Cost of Processes (ABM)

The bulleted items below and on the following pages will read like sound bites. They are written more for quick overview than for depth. These rapid-fire observations are becoming prevalent in many business magazines, so you as the reader will also have to be a thought-integrator.

- As organizations flatten in structure and companies strengthen their commitment to customer satisfaction and customer retention, business processes are becoming more visible. Business processes run across artificial organizational boundaries, and they are emerging in full view of all managers' eyes as the vehicles that bring and achieve value for customers. Some business processes are part of the supplier value chain. The supply chain is what needs to be better managed. Activity accounting quantifies this new view with cost data.
- Customers are gaining in power. Brand loyalty is declining and giving way to everyday low prices and a keener sense for value. Customers are also seeking increased customization to meet their unique needs. There is no "average" customer. This creates

greater product variety and diversity along with new services. Business is no longer some sort of anonymous distribution system through which to pump products.

- Organizations are discovering that the business process performance levels necessary to remain competitive exceed what is possible from conventional, highly vertical, functional organization forms. The traditional corporate model is becoming less valid as business processes transcend the old departmental boundaries. Future cost reductions and performance improvements can be achieved only through reconfiguring work activities into fewer, more integrated jobs. Optimizing a functional department is nonoptimal.

- The major, core cross-functional business processes of any organization are large in size and few in number. Examples of business processes are order fulfillment (from customer order to cash payment) or new product development (from concept idea to final prototype). They are best expressed as from "point to point" (refer to Figure 1–6). Having only a few core processes simplifies an employee's grasp on their perceived complexity. (Note: Manufacturing processes are relatively mature and are imbedded inside the order fulfillment business processes.)

- Functional names, like an Order Entry Department, disguise the broader business processes. In contrast, groups of activities, like those occurring in research and development, are often not recognized as core business processes.

- Customers see increasing value in good business processes and will pay a premium for them. For example, Federal Express' overnight delivery and McDonald's ready-to-serve meals revolutionized their industries.

- Traditional financial accounting supports old-fashioned functional (i.e., boundaried stovepipe and silo) thinking. When you tilt the organization sideways 90 degrees and begin thinking in terms of process and not function, then the financial accounting system becomes an obstacle. Here are the two major problems:
  - The chart-of-accounts (e.g., wages, fringe benefits, supplies, etc.) gives no visibility to work, to work's content, and to work's worth to customers. To overcome this deficiency, activity accounting forces the use of verb-noun grammar so

FIGURE 1-6

Point-to-Point Nature of the Process-Based Approach

The organization chart is being replaced by process-based thinking.

- Business processes run *across* artificial organizational boundaries.

- ABC/ABM *quantifies* and helps people *visualize* business processes.

- Business processes are large in scope and few in number.

Processes usually start and end with a customer and have point-to-point naming such as from a customer order to customer payment.

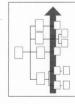

that employees can finally *see* the work—and employees are actually more comfortable with this more natural language of activities (see Figure 1–7).

- Departmental or cost center segmented financial reporting perpetuates the vertical hierarchy as the driving force in an organization, instead of the more deserving customer who is at the end of a business process crossing the organization horizontally.

- A significant challenge will surface as process-based cost reporting and associated performance measures take root. There will be tension between those who will continue to support functional organizational goals and those wishing to meet customer needs. In many organizations the neighbors don't trust one another. In customer-focused companies, they behave like a unified community.

- Traditional accounting blocks managers from seeing, under-standing, and reacting to the costs they should be managing. It blocks them from understanding the causes of their costs. In contrast, activity accounting brings visibility. It also brings quantification. ABC/ABM connects action words to management concepts and vice versa. It shows end-users where accountability and empowerment intersect. It is a mirror reflection of the organization's costs of business processes.

- Both process owners and participants will need cost data that support this new end-to-end horizontal thinking. New organizational alignments to support customers will exhibit cen-tralized control with decentralized execution. The former requires better cost planning; the latter, more relevant cost monitoring.

- Activity accounting provides a natural framework to assign value. Where are we adding value? Where are we not adding value? Where should we be adding value? How well are we adding value? These questions can be answered by scoring or grading the value-content of individual activities within supply chain processes.

- Total quality management (TQM) teams and just-in-time (JIT) cycle-time compression teams are taught to think in terms of processes and to measure processes. With some outdated business processes, encrusted with a legacy of path-dependent, quick-fix

Shortcomings of General Ledger Reporting

Stating activities in an action verb–object noun convention creates an atmosphere for change by providing people with a new way of looking at something they are already familiar with, rather than something foreign.

From: General Ledger

Chart-of-Accounts View

Claims Processing Department

	Actual	Plan	Favorable/ (Unfavorable)
Salaries	$621,4000	$600,000	$(21,400)
Equipment	161,200	150,000	(11,200)
Travel expenses	58,000	60,000	2,000
Supplies	43,900	40,000	(3,900)
Use and occupancy	30,000	30,000	—
Total	$914,500	$880,000	(34,500)

To: ABC Database

Activity-Based View

Claims Processing Department

Key/scan claims	$31,500
Analyze claims	121,000
Suspend claims	32,500
Received provider inquiries	101,500
Resolve membership problems	83,400
Process batches	45,000
Determine eligibility	119,000
Make copies	145,500
Write correspondence	77,100
Attend training	158,000
Total	$914,500

When managers get this kind of report, they are either happy or sad, but they are rarely any smarter.

corrections, TQM and JIT teams are now running into walls, namely themselves. Their efforts are not always turning into benefits or improving profits. Senior management is getting disturbed by the diminishment of benefits realized from TQM.

- Why examine activities? Examining activities helps employees understand activities, which in turn enables them to affect activities. Also, the root causes that drive activity costs can be identified and included in employees' thinking. This is all very human and behavioral. Remember that activities ultimately always involve people serving other people. The idea is to positively influence behavior. And that means not penalizing people for errors, but discouraging them from the repetition of errors (see Figure 1–8).

Only activity-based accounting principles support process-based thinking and its associated business improvement actions and programs. Activities are such a central foundation. TQM is doing activities without errors. JIT is doing activities without waste. Reengineering is synchronizing activities across functional boundaries. With traditional accounting there is no process view; you can't get there from here. With activity accounting, you can follow the path of a business process. And you can check the alignment of costs with senior management's defined strategies.

1–3B. Product and Service Costs (ABC)

- Allocations are out. Direct costing is in. Just say no to allocations! Here's why:
  - Complexity and product/service diversity are escalating. Unique customer needs are driving this explosion. Meeting customer needs is resulting in increasing overhead costs, but the majority of those overhead costs can be causally traced to whom (which customer) or to what (which product) the overhead activity work is benefiting. When redistributing costs, accountants call the *whom* and the *what* the final cost objects.
  - Ideally, all costs should be directly charged, but as technology increases, more costs are indirect. Activity-based costing acts as a surrogate for directly charging costs of activities that traditionally have not been traced to cost objects. ABC

The Role of Work Activities

Why examine activities?

- People easily understand activities.

- Activities can be actionably affected.

- Activities highlight the root causes that drive costs.

- Combining activities with their cost drivers improves the accuracy of cost objects (like product costs).

- Activities integrate time, cost, and quality performance measures with process-based thinking and improvement projects.

Employees

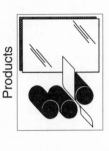

Products

Output

displaces the traditional and distorting practice of allocating ("spreading like peanut butter") expenses. Allocations should be a last resort. Figure 1–9 illustrates this.

- Traditional financial accounting practices inadequately capture how the diversity of products and services consume resources via the activities that serve them. Figure 1–10 pictures various types of diversities. Allocations are bad because:
  - Allocations assume convenient or arbitrary ways, and certainly uncorrelated ways, to assign costs.
  - Allocations apply *averaging* (e.g., a cost/event or cost/time period burden rate) when in fact product or service cost consumption patterns are actually irregular and dispropor- tionate. A broad-brush average hardly represents the unique population of consuming cost objects. (In practice, some infrastructure-sustaining costs that are fixed in the short-term may need to be allocated, but it depends on the end-user's use of the cost data. This will be discussed in Section 3–4.)

Figure 1–11 pictures how ABC more realistically traces the flow of costs. The collective impact of all forms of diversity are eventually captured in the final cost objects.

- As a consequence of unquestioned formula cost allocations, traditional financial accounting can grotesquely distort the true costs of products and services, which in turn can wildly distort their individual profit margins. Total costs are being redistributed in what is effectively a zero-sum and no-net-change game. Only ABC adequately removes the distortions from simplistic cost allocations (see Figure 1–12). An allocation-free cost system is like a smoke-free environment—no pollution. In short, don't allocate—prorate. In sum, ABC serves as a *direct-costing* system for the *total* enterprise.

Once the product or service costs are accurately calculated, then the fun really begins. Figure 1–13 shows how the ABC profit margins are in- dividually calculated. Since it is predictable that hidden losses exist as a result of historical misguided pricing, it follows that ABC will ultimately reveal with what specific products, services, and customers are profits or losses really occurring. Reassigning costs is a zero-sum game. But cost- plus pricing linked to the traditional costs creates a total net profit condi- tion of big winners or big losers.

FIGURE 1-9

The Flow of Costs

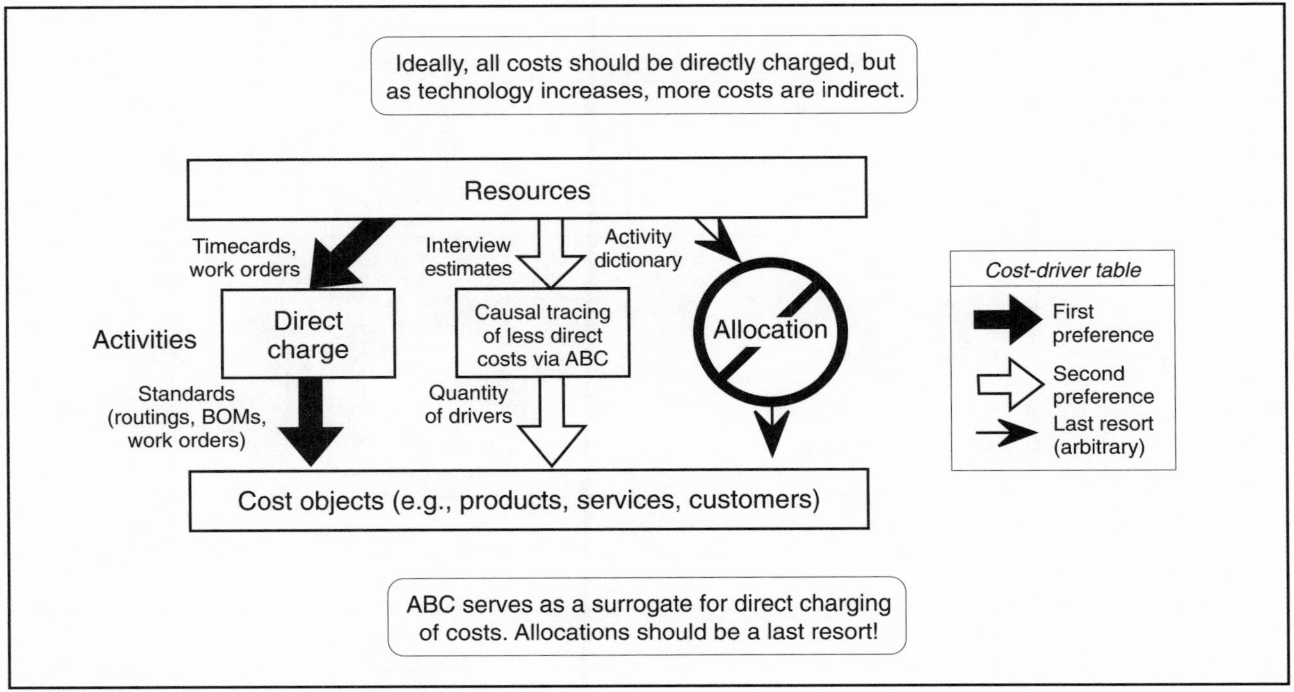

Ideally, all costs should be directly charged, but as technology increases, more costs are indirect.

Resources

Activities

Timecards, work orders

Interview estimates

Activity dictionary

Direct charge

Causal tracing of less direct costs via ABC

Allocation

Standards (routings, BOMs, work orders)

Quantity of drivers

Cost objects (e.g., products, services, customers)

ABC serves as a surrogate for direct charging of costs. Allocations should be a last resort!

Cost-driver table

First preference

Second preference

Last resort (arbitrary)

F I G U R E 1-10

Product Costs and Varieties

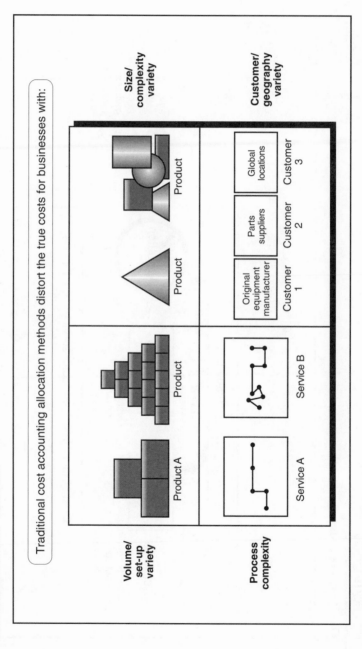

FIGURE 1-11

Flowing Costs to Segment Diversity

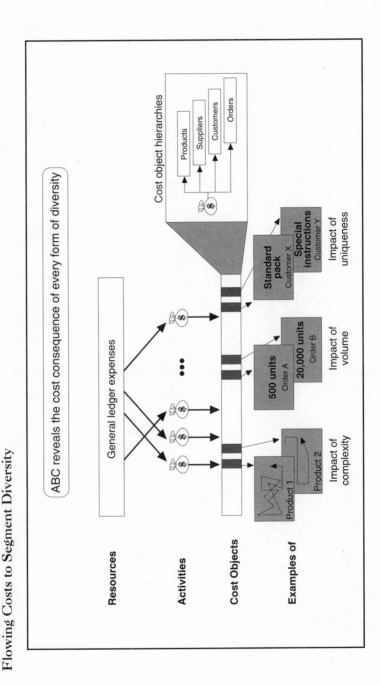

FIGURE 1-12

ABC Squeezes Out Cost Distortions

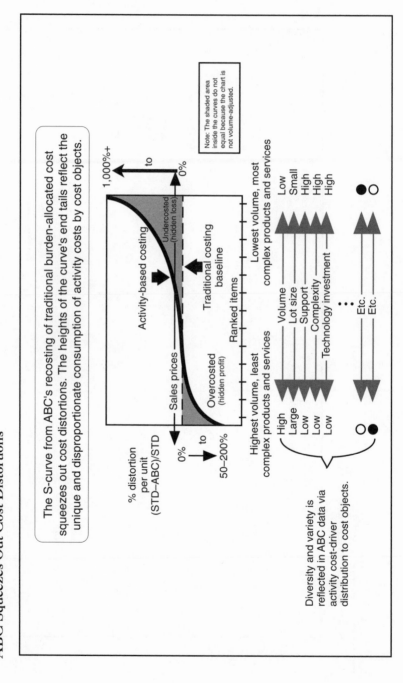

The S-curve from ABC's recosting of traditional burden-allocated cost squeezes out cost distortions. The heights of the curve's end tails reflect the unique and disproportionate consumption of activity costs by cost objects.

Note: The shaded area inside the curves do not equal because the chart is not volume-adjusted.

1,000%+

to

0%

% distortion per unit (STD–ABC)/STD

0%

to

50–200%

Activity-based costing

Undercosted (hidden loss)

Traditional costing baseline

Sales prices

Overcosted (hidden profit)

Ranked items

Highest volume, least complex products and services

Lowest volume, most complex products and services

Volume
Lot size
Support
Complexity
Technology investment

High
Large
Low
Low
Low

Low
Small
High
High
High

Etc.
Etc.

Diversity and variety is reflected in ABC data via activity cost-driver distribution to cost objects.

FIGURE 1-13

Calculation of ABC Profit Margins

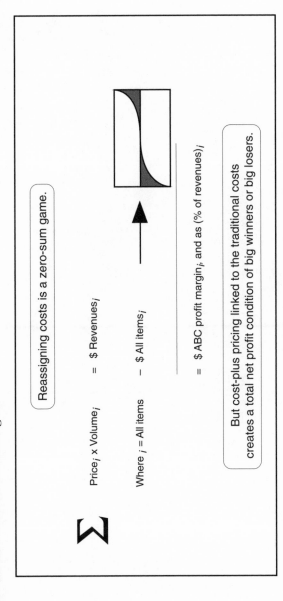

Reassigning costs is a zero-sum game.

$\sum$

$Price_i \times Volume_i \quad = \$ Revenues_i$

$Where\ i = All\ items \quad - \$ All\ items_i$

$= \$ ABC\ profit\ margin_i,\ and\ as\ (\%\ of\ revenues)_i$

But cost-plus pricing linked to the traditional costs creates a total net profit condition of big winners or big losers.

FIGURE 1-14

Example of a Profitability Profile

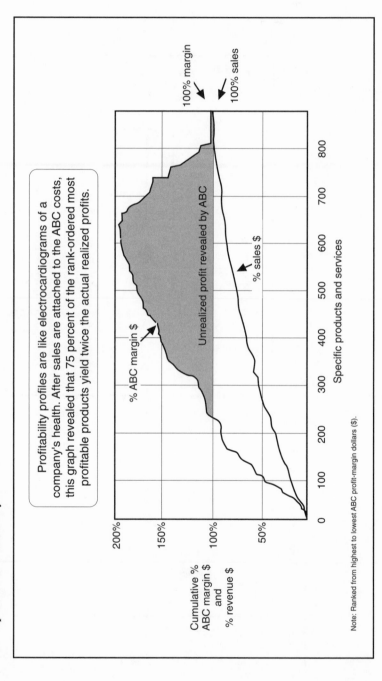

Profitability profiles are like electrocardiograms of a company's health. After sales are attached to the ABC costs, this graph revealed that 75 percent of the rank-ordered most profitable products yield twice the actual realized profits.

100% margin
100% sales

% ABC margin $

Unrealized profit revealed by ABC

% sales $

Cumulative %
ABC margin $
and
% revenue $

200%

150%

100%

50%

0   100   200   300   400   500   600   700   800

Specific products and services

Note: Ranked from highest to lowest ABC profit-margin dollars ($).

With ABC profit margins now computed, a graph plotting the highest to lowest (i.e., losses) ABC margin dollars can be plotted like Figure 1–14. The shock comes from seeing that a much greater profit than ever considered was captured by perhaps two-thirds of the more profitable products—and then there were big losses!

In sum, profitability computations that combine customers with more accurately costed products and services is an advanced measure. It helps management locate profit-friendly customers and grow more of those kind. It also helps managers to suggest how some of their unprofitable customers can alter their own behavior to become profitable. In the extreme case it helps managers terminate some of their customers.

ABC is about segmenting the diversity of consumed resources and logically tracing them to the products, services, and customers. Can traditional unit-volume-based overhead cost allocation methods work? Only if your business has the characteristics like in Figure 1–15.

ABC/ABM data do not provide a panacea. Costs are a symptom, not the root cause. Arguably ABC/ABM is not in the same category as other performance improvement programs. However, better cost data can serve as enablers and initiative accelerators to those programs. Cost information reinforces the thinking needed to make improvement programs really work. *Costs measure effect, not cause.* But with data on cost-driver

FIGURE   1–15

Traditional Cost Allocation Is Obsolete

Traditional cost allocation methods work when . . .

- Few very similar products/services.
- Low overhead.
- Homogenous producing/conversion processes.
- Homogenous customers, customer demands, and marketing channels.
- Low selling, distribution, and administrative costs.
- Very high margins.

Any company you know?

rates also being an output of an ABC/ABM model, managers can visibly quantify and rationalize the causes of cost. And by understanding the relative magnitude of graded attributes that are attached to activity costs (e.g., low-value added), and the impact of individual activity costs for recent time periods, managers and employees can improve their focus on where the good improvement opportunities are.

1–3C. Target Costing

Ideally, prices should be linked to sensitivities of customers and the market. Too often, marked-up costs are computed to ensure a profit margin. Target costing, which is price-based, offers an improvement over cost-based pricing.

In Japan, cost management is the responsibility of engineers, not accountants (which ironically is where the responsibility historically was located in the United States in the 1920s at the beginning of the Industrial Revolution). The Japanese treat costs as a symptom, not a cause or a solution. But they embrace cost symptoms as important clues for tackling problems or seeking opportunities.

Target costing begins with the assumption of the customer's ability to pay. That is, it begins with market-based pricing independent of cost. And since earning a profit is considered as a given, then a target cost becomes a calculated number that cannot be exceeded during the product's design:

Target cost = Market-priced sales – Target profit

Manufacturers in most countries outside Japan usually first design and produce their products, and then they calculate a cost-plus markup to determine a selling price. Salespeople then hope there is a market for the product at that price:

Actual cost + Planned profit = Price

Figure 1–16 reveals the intrinsic benefits of the target-costing approach. Costs are best managed during the concept and design phase when engineers can be restricted to "live within the company's means" to develop a marketable product. And by excelling in strong and stable designs, the engineers are effectively committing the costs up front. Costs are intrinsically created early during the new product or service development phase.

There is a time lag between product design decisions and their impact on operating costs. Cost causes and cost occurrences are separated by time.

FIGURE 1–16

Costs Are Committed in the Concept and Design Phases

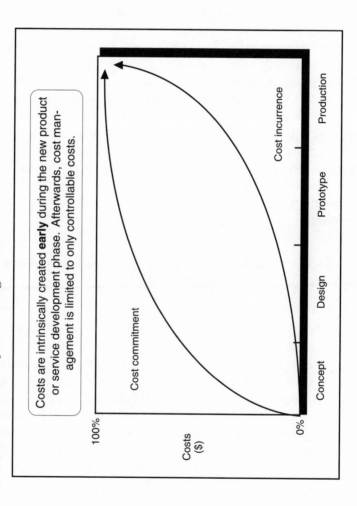

Costs are intrinsically created **early** during the new product or service development phase. Afterwards, cost management is limited to only controllable costs.

29

Without stable designs, the frequency and intensity of engineering design changes that can follow will generate excessive costs later in the product's life cycle. Figure 1–17 shows how Japanese cost management starts with target costing and finishes with *kaizen* during the subsequent production phase. In contrast, other countries focus on managing (i.e., beating up) the production personnel to get costs in line. Generally, production and operations face a predicament: they can only increase costs, by introducing some level of inefficiency, but they cannot substantially reduce costs outside the constraints of the predetermined product (and associated process) designs.

ABC/ABM systems are a result of the competitive business need for much sharper pencils than ever needed before. ABC/ABM data bring cost visibility of business processes where there was none and bring greater accuracy to product and service costs where today there are large errors. In some circles, applying ABC for product costing has been called "feature-based costing." The design features govern the amount of activity cost usage. It is consistent with ABC concepts. Figure 1–18 summarizes today's thoughts about traditional financial accounting.

1–3D. Full Absorption Costing with Fixed versus Variable Thinking

- All costs are variable in the long run. That includes your job.
- When tracing costs to activities, products, or services, it can be dangerous to excessively include certain kinds of costs (e.g., lawn-cutting services). When costs that are outside the control of managers and employees are recklessly included (e.g., total cost per unit of output), without any indicator or caveat, it sends misleading signals to managers and employees. It can convey that if they reduce certain costs, other allocated costs will automatically be reduced too. They won't. Many overhead costs are consumed without any direct relation to the traditional cost allocation basis. This section discusses the economic behavior of costs.
- Few costs are actually fixed, that is, permanent (excluding capital purchases, which are sunk costs). Costs are commonly referred to as fixed if they do not vary in proportion or if they do not parallel some level of sales or production volume. In reality, most activity

FIGURE 1-17

Comparison of Japanese and U.S. Cost Management

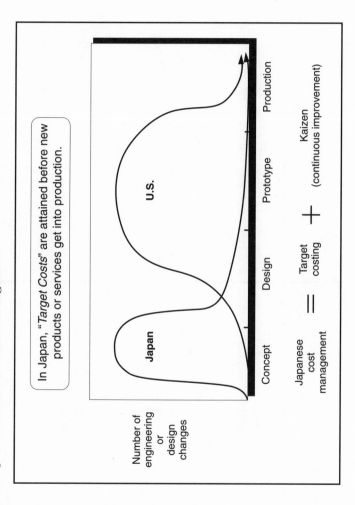

FIGURE 1-18

Shortcomings of Traditional Financial Accounting

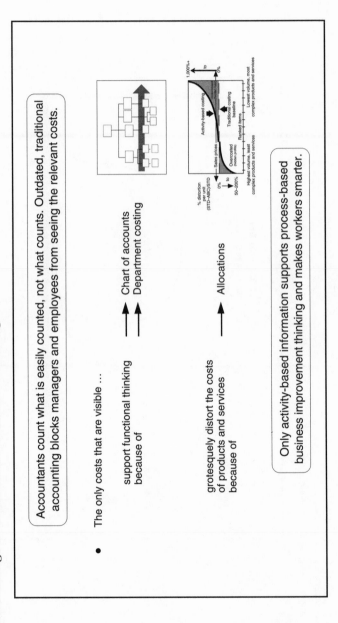

Accountants count what is easily counted, not what counts. Outdated, traditional accounting blocks managers and employees from seeing the relevant costs.

- The only costs that are visible …

  support functional thinking because of → Chart of accounts
  → Department costing

  grotesquely distort the costs of products and services because of → Allocations

Only activity-based information supports process-based business improvement thinking and makes workers smarter.

costs either vary with some type of nonsales, nonproduction activity cost driver (e.g., number of phone calls, number of tests) or they can be partitioned to reflect how they serve a specific product family, customer segment, or class of purchased supplies or subcontractor's services. When these cost drivers or the beneficiaries of the activities go away, so do the work activities and eventually their costs (refer to Figure 1–19).

- Traditional accounting "unitizes" costs, giving the illusion that all of the costs directly vary with units of end output (or input such as labor hours in). The focus should be on total costs per time period, not cost per unit. If the units of output go away, not much of the unitized costs go away. Do not leave impressions that they do. Traditional accounting sends bad and misleading signals.

- Only ABC/ABM principles provide the capability to focus on total costs while specifically capturing which activity costs vary with a unique cost driver to benefit a family/class/segment of a product, service, or customer—and to what degree those costs vary.

- Unused capacity costs should not flow through to cost objects (e.g., products or services). Such surplus resources that are deemed below expected demand levels should be isolated and traced to an "unused capacity activity." Otherwise, by their inclusion, one penalizes product marketing teams with an unfair burden not borne by their competitors. Surplus capacity often results from prior management's misjudgments about expected demand or resources needed to meet demand. It is management's responsibility for either removing the surplus or finding a productive use for it. Section 5–2 further discusses this subject.

- Only ABC/ABM principles allow declaring some costs like building rent as being fixed (with regard to a relevant time-range) or as being discretionary. This facilitates separately reporting certain uncontrollable costs as a "company tax or surcharge," rather than traditional accounting's practice of baking those costs directly into process, product, or service costs. Doing so misleads users into thinking that those costs are controllable or vary in tandem with the output rates of processes, products, or services. There is very little connection.

FIGURE 1-19

Full Absorption Costing

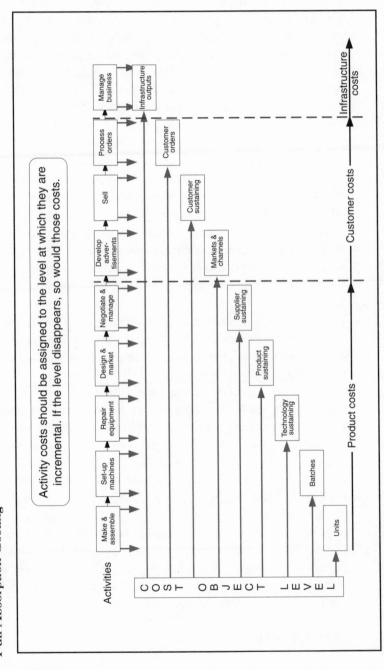

Activity costs should be assigned to the level at which they are incremental. If the level disappears, so would those costs.

Source: *The Complete Guide to Activity-Based Costing*, page 91, by Michael O'Guinn, © 1991. Used by permission of Prentice Hall/Career & Personal Development.

1–3E. The Annual Budget Death March

There are criticisms about the use and development of expense budgets. Some companies are saying they want cost management, not budget management. Why bother to budget? What are the origins of budgeting? The simple answer is that owners and senior managers have always needed some form of control to responsibly match spending with funding.

Historically, the most convenient way to restrict managers from spending and to prevent excesses or abuses was to start with the official financial reporting mechanism, the general ledger. The general ledger reported the big profit-and-loss picture; the next step was to disaggregate its spending accounts into its constituent parts, conveniently the departments, which in turn could be further disaggregated again and again. This is depicted in Figure 1–20. By assigning spending targets using the same classifications as the actual financial reporting, namely the general ledger chart of accounts, the budget effectively mirrored total companywide financial spending and funding.

With hindsight, we now realize the budget is a mirror of the organization chart, not the business processes. And worse, the budget has no visibility to the content of work and no provisions to logically determine how external or internal cost drivers govern the natural levels of spending caused by demands on work.

Here are further observations:

- Today's budget process takes an extraordinarily long time, sometimes exceeding a year, while during the process the organization reshuffles and resizes. In addition, customers and competitors usually change their behavior for which oftentimes a prudent reaction cannot be accommodated in the budget.
- Low cost is a dependent variable; it's the result of doing other things well. You cannot budget your way into low-cost operations. Budget management and cost management are not synonymous.
- The loudest voice, the greatest political muscle, or the largest budget are no longer valid ways to manage resources.
- The annual budget is a sacred cow in some companies, and generally the effort of producing it hardly outweighs the benefits it supposedly yields.

FIGURE 1-20

Disaggregation of the General Ledger

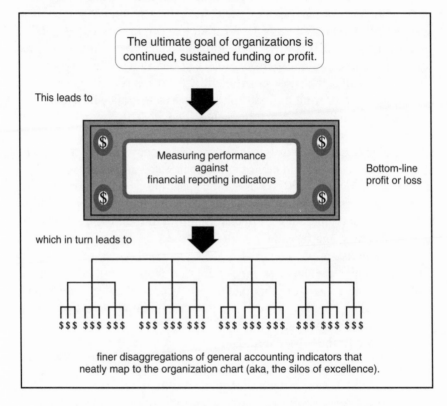

- Budgets are useful for businesses that are stable and in which senior management does not trust their organization to intelligently spend money. Both of those conditions are invalid today.
- Many companies confuse budgeting (the spending control club) with financial planning (the forecaster). Computer models today can forecast the outcomes of all sorts of assumption-based scenarios without the need of the formal budget exercise. Businesses need to experiment with financial simulators before they spend the hard dollars.
- Budget should reflect strategy. Strategies should be formulated at two levels. First, the diversification strategy level answers, *"What*

should we be doing?" Second, the business strategy level asks, "*How* should we do it?" Unfortunately, most of the effort is on the latter question, and companies get preoccupied with simply finishing the budget.

- Often the budget is revised midyear or more frequently with forecasts. Then there is an excess amount of attention given to analyzing differences—all the differences. These include budget-to-forecast, last-forecast-to-current-forecast, actual-to-budget, actual-to-forecast, and on and on.

- Often the budget numbers that roll up from lower- and mid-level managers mislead the organization because of sandbagging (i.e., padding) by the managers. "Use it or lose it" is standard practice of managers during the last fiscal quarter. Budgets can be an invitation to some managers to spend needlessly.

- Budgets can be demotivating if they are either too easy or too challenging.

Figure 1–21 is a tongue-in-cheek survey. How does your organization measure up?

FIGURE 1–21

Annual Budget Survey

```
┌─────────────────────────────────────────────────────────────────────┐
│                                                                      │
│                  ┌─────────────────────────────────┐                 │
│                  │  The Annual Budgeting Exercise . . . │             │
│                  └─────────────────────────────────┘                 │
│                                                                      │
│   ☐  Is a death march with few benefits.                             │
│                                                                      │
│   ☐  Takes 14 months start-to-end.                                   │
│                                                                      │
│   ☐  Requires two or more executive adjustments.                     │
│                                                                      │
│   ☐  Is obsolete in two months due to reorganizations and unplanned  │
│      reactions to competitor moves and market behavior.              │
│                                                                      │
│   ☐  Strangles needed spending while tolerating unrecognized excesses│
│      elsewhere.                                                      │
│                                                                      │
│   ☐  Penalizes downstream victims caused by pollution upstream in    │
│      the business processes.                                         │
│                                                                      │
│   ☐  All six of the above.                                           │
│                                                                      │
└─────────────────────────────────────────────────────────────────────┘
```

- Activity-based accounting mechanics effectively model the resource consumption rates and patterns of an enterprise on a cross-functional business process basis. Hence, ABC-type budgets can be regenerated at periodic intervals based on estimates of the quantities of activity cost drivers in combination with the precomputed rates of activity cost drivers.

1–3F. The Decline of Standard Cost Accounting Systems?

- ABC/ABM is in effect an expanded version of a standard cost accounting system. The major difference is that the ABC/ABM model more logically segregates spending pools and matches each pool to an activity cost driver that truly mirrors and parallels the consumption rate and cost behavior of that spending pool. Remember, ABC/ABM is intended to be allocation-free.
- If you can imagine infinite computing power and a virtually cost- and effort-free way to record and collect agreed-upon relevant data, don't standard cost practices go away? Remember, this equation always holds: actual equals the standard +/– the variance. Assuming our hypothetical computing and reporting scenario, frequently reported "actual" data encourage trend monitoring, not red-flag alerts to exceptions based on stale and oftentimes flawed averages.
- Figure 1–22 reveals that as a company incurs constant changes from its mix of customer orders and improvements to its processes, the magnitude of activity costs fluctuate. The standard cost system establishes a "cross-hair telescope" baseline using history for the standard, and then actual data is compared to assess the deviation from standard. Oftentimes, the baseline measure is what is flawed, not the actual result. As more rapid, frequent actual data collection occurs (which is like going from freeze-frame to rolling cinema), over time users will remember prior baselines and effectively adopt trend-line analysis based on frequent absolute measures, not deviations from preset standards.

FIGURE 1-22

Decline of Standard Cost

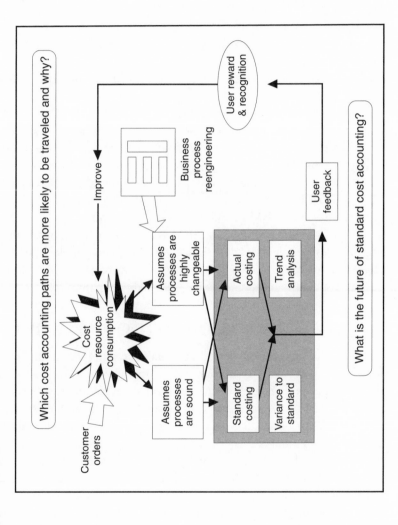

1–4. CLARIFYING WHAT ABC, ABCM, AND ABM ARE

There is significant confusion about the semantics and acronyms associated with activity-based information for which no standard definitions exist. Figure 1–23 places three levels of activity-based information on a graph, relating them to organizational impact.

In a narrow sense, activity-based costing (ABC) can be considered the mathematics used to reassign costs accurately to cost objects, that is, outputs, products, services, customers. Its primary purpose is for profitability analysis.

Activity-based cost management (ABCM) uses the ABC cost information to not only rationalize what products or services to sell but, more important, to identify opportunities to change the activities and processes to improve productivity.

Activity-based management (ABM) integrates ABC and ABCM with noncost metrics such as cycle time, quality, agility, flexibility, and customer service. ABM goes beyond cost information.

ABCM and ABM overlap. ABM is the more popular acronym used in regard to leveraging ABC data. Since ABCM is less popular, this book will restrict its reference to only ABC and ABM; however, ABM will primarily have a cost-centric meaning. Figure 1–24 adds definitions for Figure 1–23.

1–5. FINAL THOUGHTS ON ABC/ABM

In a nutshell, this chapter described what is creating the multiple and various interests for activity accounting. Companies need to see the content of work and predict the potential impact on work of new customer orders, decisions, and proposed improvement projects and initiatives. Companies need to better understand the creation of value. The traditional general ledger financial accounting system requires a translation into an activity-based language with new metrics. Computing costs with ABC/ABM is relatively mechanical. Dealing with people, their lack of understanding of costs, and their resistance to new ways of looking at the same world they operate in is the more difficult implementation challenge. Success will not come until the attitudes of individuals are changed. Only after that happens will shared group values emerge.

FIGURE 1-23

Activity-Based Information Acronyms

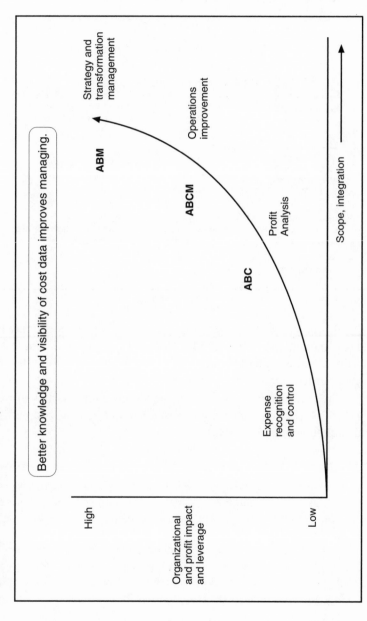

F I G U R E   1–24

ABM versus ABCM versus ABC

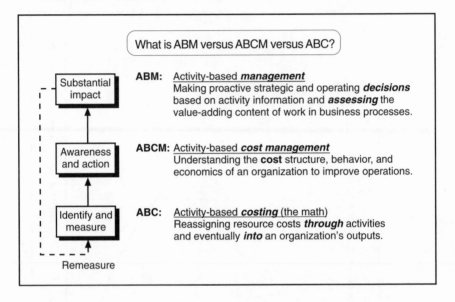

To many organizations, simple rules for improvement may be satisfactory, particularly if they are far from performing well. But those organizations will eventually need ABC/ABM when they think they are getting closer to optimum performance.

The next chapter expands on the softer, human issues of overcoming ABC/ABM implementation obstacles and getting people on board and excited about ABC/ABM.

The question may well be asked: To what extent are cost records actually brought to the attention of foremen . . .? Our experience (shows that) management keeps cost data closely guarded and usually does not want the foremen to know. . . .

Many foremen have risen from the ranks. . . . As a class they do not realize that whenever they endeavor to find a reason for doing a certain thing . . ., they are searching for a theory. The dominant characteristics of any group of foremen are likely to be as follows:

■ They have well-established habits.

- They are largely "self-made" men.

- They are self-confident and of the "show-me" type.

- They are usually not entirely open-minded.

- They think best in the face of opposition.

- They keenly enjoy discussing their everyday problems.

- They have high regard for the square deal.

This whole question (of providing foremen with cost data) is one of the most important confronting the cost accountant, the solution of which can materially advance the progress of American industry.

Hugo Diemer[2]

---

2. Hugo Diemer, "Methods of Supplying Cost Information to Foremen," *National Association of Cost Accountants (NACA) Bulletin,* vol. 5, no. 18, June 1, 1921.

CHAPTER 2

Why Some ABC/ABM Systems Fail

Many cost systems have failed to accomplish the desired results because
they were installed without an adequate conception of the problems
involved or the factors that should have been considered.

H. G. Crockett[1]

The reality about ABC/ABM implementations is sobering because their
success rate has been below what one would expect. These failures are
surprising, considering the poor grades that most employees and managers give their existing traditional cost system data. Figure 2–1 displays
three possible paths that ABC/ABM projects can follow. Only one path
breaks above the "project combustion level" indicating sustained success. From the beginning point, all three paths initially turn upward on
unbridled enthusiasm and optimism, but then they diverge. Two paths result in failure. Only one path leads to success. Let's travel along each
path and learn from experience.

2–1. THE PATH TO ABC/ABM SUCCESS

The *lowest path* drops downward into "the valley of despair" following
employee disillusion with the ABC/ABM project and the resulting drop
in interest and support. The reasons are described below. Since the direction toward process-based managing techniques is inevitable, these
ABC/ABM projects will eventually reemerge from their dormant state.
Renewed or resurrected ABC/ABM projects can possibly result from a
turnover in managers or too many unplanned surprises, that is, bad and
costly decisions caused by the existing traditional accounting system.

The *middle path* reflects strong individuals who continue to champion the virtues of ABC/ABM thinking. The power of their strong

---

1. H. G. Crockett, "Some Problems in the Actual Installation of Cost Systems," *National Association
   of Cost Accountants (NACA) Bulletin,* vol. 1, no. 8, February 1921.

Possible Paths of ABC/ABM Projects

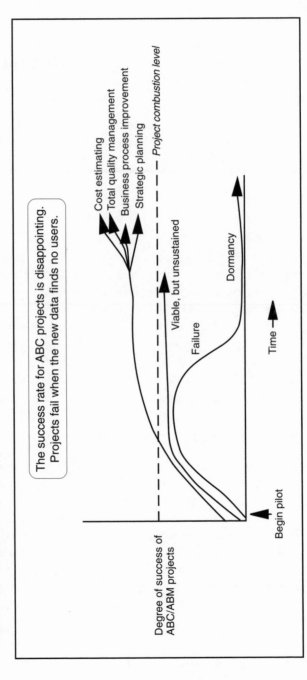

personalities keeps the ABC/ABM implementation project afloat. Unfortunately, the usefulness of the new cost data they produce has not been sufficiently recognized by employees to break above that combustion level for success, where any project or system takes off on its own merits.

The *top path* represents the successful ABC/ABM projects that are pulled through by the unabashed interests of individuals to use the data to do their jobs better and make better decisions. What prevents many ABC/ABM projects from attaining this top path? Learning from the failures of previous implementors of ABC/ABM will increase the chance for future success.

2–2. CAUSES FOR ABC/ABM FAILURES

A good approach is to not repeat mistakes of others and to correct for why many other ABC/ABM projects have stumbled. Unfortunately, there are so many reasons that ABC/ABM projects have had difficulties that it is probably more useful to divide the problems into four broad categories based on the severity:

- The biggies, or showstoppers
- The user rejections
- The organizational obstacles
- The nuisances

The biggies, or showstoppers, summarized in Figure 2–2, are:

- When ABC/ABM projects are launched from the finance or accounting department (or are excessively staffed by accountants), they are usually perceived by those that the project is intended to help as another meaningless financial or managerial exercise.
- Financial accounting tends to be "outside the comfort zone" of most individuals. The new accounting data cannot be forced upon potential users.
- The new ABC/ABM initiative is routinely approached without predefining tangible, results-oriented objectives. That is, the ABC/ABM model or system was installed with a "Field of Dreams" illusion as in the recent Hollywood movie: "if we (the ABC/ABM project team) build it, they (the data users) will come." That is nonsense. They won't come if there were no problem sets earlier identified for the new data to better solve.

FIGURE 2-2

Causes for Implementation Failure

> **Why has ABC/ABM sometimes failed?**
> **The "biggies" reasons are:**

- The project was launched from finance, not pulled through from operations.
- Cost accounting is outside most everyone's comfort zones.
- The system was installed like a "Field of Dreams," without a predefined problem for the data to solve and with no stated objective.
- It competes with the official regulatory accounting system as a parallel and off-line information system.
- There is an underestimated degree of employee resistance to change and of corporate disbelief with the new costs.
- The ABC/ABM system is overdesigned with detail and flunks too many "closeness beats precision" tests.

Source: David E. Keys, Household International Professor of Cost Management, Northern Illinois University; assisted by Gary Cokins, 1995.

- There is an impression that simply computing the new ABC/ABM data for users is a gracious act. Without a plan, even if people look at the data, they will learn a lot, but they won't necessarily get anything done.
- The ABC/ABM information becomes "a second set of books," thus competing with the "official" accounting system. Employee performance measures are often linked to the official system, which can consequently encourage bad behavior. And with two sets of cost numbers, people get caught up reconciling the differences.
- The magnitude of resistance to change is grossly underestimated. Business people not trained in financial accounting tend to think a successful accounting system is one that regularly generates financial reports or that balances the financial books monthly. They ask, "What's broken if the system achieves those results each month?"
- The degree of disbelief of the newly calculated numbers is always underestimated by the ABC/ABM project team. With accurate tracing of costs, the resulting costs of certain products,

services, or process outputs can differ dramatically from their costs as allocated in traditional methods. The organizational shock is substantial.

- Some parties are adversely affected by ABC. For example, product line managers responsible for products with marginal profitability as calculated with the traditional allocation data will balk when they recognize that the ABC calculations can further shift costs into their products and therefore make their products unprofitable.

- The design of the ABC/ABM system is overengineered, excessively detailed, or flawed in some manner such that the data are not viewed as useful. Credibility is compromised. The system design flunks the "closeness beats precision" test too many times. Other flaws include poorly defining the activities without a verb-noun grammar convention, using too many activity cost drivers, or not identifying the true cost objects that consume activities.

Users might reject an ABC/ABM system (refer to Figure 2–3) because of the following:

- Sales and marketing personnel do not know how to react nor take appropriate actions once they are confronted with the new winners and losers of profitability, whether they be products, services, or customers.

FIGURE   2 – 3

Causes for Implementation Failure

> Why has ABC/ABM sometimes failed?
> The "user rejection" reasons:

- Sales and marketing personnel do not know how to react to the new profit winners and losers.
- ABC/ABM does not provide *all* the information needed to make customer and product decisions.
- ABC/ABM competes with other improvement programs without integration.
- Acting on the data involves pain—refocused strategies usually require some different people and equipment, implying job eliminations and write-offs.

Source: Adapted from William Boone, Strategic Systems Group, 1995.

- ABC/ABM does not provide all the information for product and customer planners to make decisions. It simply reflects the disproportionate and diverse consumption of resources in terms of costs. It sheds little light, for example, on the potential that customers might bring to future market or product migration strategies, or where existing products or markets are in their life cycle. Much, much more information is used by managers to decide on customer- and product-related actions.
- The ABC/ABM project is viewed as another competing improvement program rather than as enabling data to aid existing improvement programs.
- Acting on the data can involve pain for somebody. The data can lead to reorganizing people and restructuring their work in different ways that may eliminate or replace some of the existing people and equipment. When work goes away, so do people.

The organizational obstacles to ABC/ABM success (refer to Figure 2–4) include these special conditions:

- A brisk pace was not maintained after the ABC/ABM project began. If ABC/ABM projects take too long, they lose momentum and people lose interest.

FIGURE 2–4

Causes for Implementation Failure

> Why has ABC/ABM sometimes failed?
> Organization obstacles:

- The project loses initial management buy-in by not maintaining a brisk pace and momentum.
- There is no true profit-and-loss responsibility at the pilot site.
- There is minimal end-product diversity, resulting in little change in individual net costs.
- Headquarters mandates ABC/ABM with standard activities and drivers, thus stifling user involvement.
- The organization has a lack of cost management expertise.
- ABC/ABM's reputation is maligned as too costly to maintain or as a wrong tool.

Source: David E. Keys, Household International Professor of Cost Management, Northern Illinois University; assisted by Gary Cokins, 1995.

- If the pilot site is strictly a cost center without profit-and-loss responsibility or not based on market-driven selling prices, people pay less attention. No one gets very excited.
- There is minimal diversity in the number or features of end products or services (i.e., final cost objects). Consequently, although the individual components of products or elements of service may be inaccurately costed, they tend to average out in total, resulting in little net change to the end cost.
- A higher-level organization unit autocratically mandates ABC/ABM. It stipulates a predefined, standard set of activity definitions. This precludes and stifles user involvement and interest.
- The organization lacks expertise with using cost management techniques to drive productivity improvement and to support decisions.
- ABC/ABM's reputation as a business improvement tool has been maligned by naysayers as being too costly or ineffective.

The smaller nuisances (refer to Figure 2–5) affecting ABC/ABM success are:

- The project team leader lacks that "fire in the belly" needed to create change.

FIGURE 2 – 5

Causes for Implementation Failure

> Why has ABC/ABM sometimes failed?
> The nuisances are:

- The project has a weak leader or team; it lacks the "fire in the belly."
- Training was inadequate or poorly timed and failed to include the right level of people.
- Activities are incongruently related with cost drivers, many of which are not the causes of cost.
- Relevant or detailed data are unavailable.
- Scope is restricted to operations cost, not total integrated value-chain cost.

Source: David E. Keys, Household International Professor of Cost Management, Northern Illinois University; assisted by Gary Cokins, 1995.

- ABC/ABM training and awareness occurs too early for the eventual internal users to benefit from.
- Activity cost drivers do not adequately reflect the consumption rate and pattern of their respective activities. There are insufficient cause-and-effect relationships between cost flows.
- Hard, measurable data, such as the number of material moves, are unavailable or inaccessible.
- The scope of the cost model is restricted only to front-line operations, thus excluding the potentially significant impact of hidden or second-order costs elsewhere in the enterprise, such as in market or product planning, in engineering, or in customer service.

In addition to understanding all of these possible causes of failure in ABC/ABM projects, the use of common sense in managing people and their expectations can help counter potential obstacles. Just knowing that these problems exist and what they are provides a major part of the solution. The intent of this book is to help you minimize the likelihood of their occurrence and to give you the remaining part of the solution: implementation know-how.

The primary lesson to be learned from all of the failures is: Do not approach ABC/ABM as a new program. There are enough programs. Hook up ABC/ABM to one of the existing wagons in your organization rather than trying to make new tracks.

To put the past problems and failures into a meaningful context, the next chapter creates an ABC/ABM framework for mapping the flow of costs (i.e., the continuous reassigning and cumulation of costs); the chapter will also help you understand the decision-making and diagnostic capabilities afforded by the new ABC/ABM framework.

ॐ

Psychologists have defined motivation as the perception of some want or goal together with the resulting drive toward achieving the want. There is a strong link between the seemingly foreign ideas of motivation and the design of accounting systems, even though the relationship may initially appear far-fetched.

Charles T. Horngren[2]

---

2. Charles T. Horngren, *Cost Accounting: A Managerial Emphasis* (Englewood Cliffs, NJ: Prentice Hall, 1977), p. 151.

CHAPTER 3

A Framework for Mapping Cost Flows

Managers are constantly faced with decisions about selling prices, variable costs, and fixed costs. Basically managers must decide how to acquire and utilize economic resources in light of some objective. Unless they can make reasonably accurate predictions about cost and revenue levels, their decisions may yield undesirable or even disastrous results.

Charles T. Horngren[1]

In the valley of the blind, even the one-eyed man is king! Professor Robert Kaplan of the Harvard Business School used those words at a cost management conference in Nashville, Tennessee, on May 18, 1994. He was implying that with limited visibility or manageable cost data problems, many companies can get by. But with a substantially more powerful costing approach like ABC/ABM, companies can make much smarter decisions and sharper assessments, and more frequently.

This chapter concentrates on what end-users of ABC/ABM information actually do with the data. What kinds of decisions do they make? What diagnostic assessments are better enabled? What kinds of cost information can be crucial for strategic or operational purposes? The chapter chronologically describes the growing interest in process design costs, which is an expansion beyond the original product and service line costing.

3–1. THE CAM-I CROSS OF ABC/ABM

In 1990, the noted author and lecturer Dr. Peter Turney and management consultant Norm Raffish created a diagram to represent an activity-based cost management framework to benefit member companies of the not-for-profit Consortium for Advanced Manufacturers-International (CAM-I). Within CAM-I, the Cost Management Systems (CMS) program has

---

1. Charles T. Horngren, *Cost Accounting: A Managerial Emphasis* (Englewood Cliffs, NJ: Prentice Hall, 1977), p. 44.

provided a forum for leading thinkers in industry, academia, and government to collectively challenge and improve cost management systems. As shown in Figure 3–1, the diagram is commonly referred to as the *CAM-I cross.*

The diagram reveals in a simple fashion that the work activities in the intersection of the cross are integral to reporting both the costs of processes and the costs of work objects. The work objects are the persons or things that benefit from incurring activity costs. Examples of final cost objects are a component part of an assembled product or a specific customer. The vertical cost assignment (ABC) direction explains what things cost and is called the cost object view, whereas the horizontal *process view* (ABM) explains why things cost and what causes costs to exist.

The vertical ABC product view is very effective at capturing how the diversity of things, like different products or various customers, can be detected and their costs reassigned by first measuring resources through their consuming activities and then into the form of final cost objects. In contrast, the horizontal ABM process view is very effective at displaying in cost terms the end-to-end alignment of activities of a business process. Since a process is defined as a sequence or network of two or more activities with a common purpose, a process' costs are additive regardless of an activity's defined level of detail. In addition, the ABM process view can provide nonfinancial, operational information about activities, such as inputs, outputs, constraints, and enablers. The ABM process view is frequently called the *supplier value-chain,* and its costs are interpreted using process value analysis (PVA). Figure 3–2 adds definitions to the CAM-I cross.

In an ABC/ABM system, the total resource costs will always reconcile to the total process costs and the total cost object costs. It is a closed cost system with dual measures that pivot around work activities. This is a key point. Traditional cost systems start with which ledger account balances get charged with an expense. In contrast, *ABC starts with work activities, not people or their wages, as the origin of thinking.* This makes ABC a socio-technical tool, not just a reporting tool.

3–2. THE PRODUCT AND SERVICE LINE VIEW (ABC)

Although today's acceptance and practice of activity accounting is being boosted by the managerial revolution toward process and systems-based

FIGURE 3-1

Multiple Cost Views

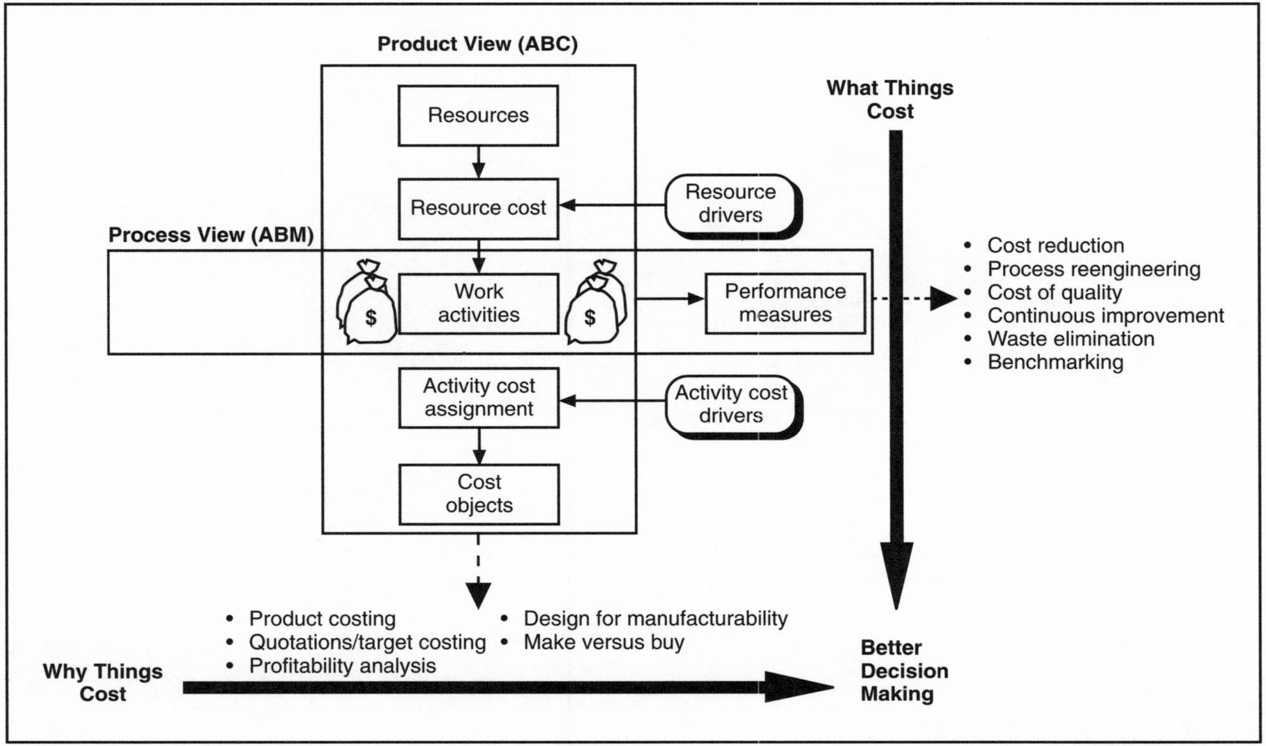

Process View (ABM)

Product View (ABC)

Resource drivers

Resources → Resource cost → Work activities

Performance measures

Activity cost drivers

Activity cost assignment → Cost objects

What Things Cost

• Cost reduction
• Process reengineering
• Cost of quality
• Continuous improvement
• Waste elimination
• Benchmarking

Better Decision Making

• Design for manufacturability
• Make versus buy

• Product costing
• Quotations/target costing
• Profitability analysis

Why Things Cost

FIGURE 3-2

Activities Are Central to Both Views

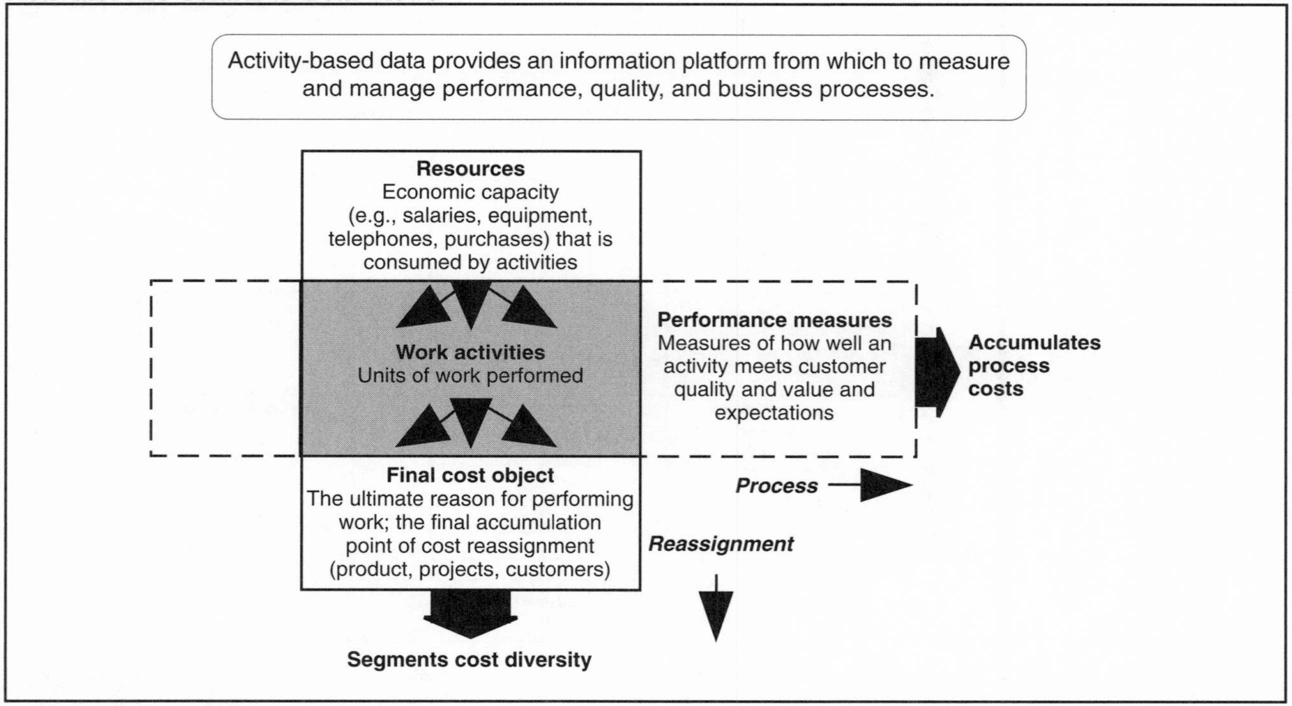

Activity-based data provides an information platform from which to measure and manage performance, quality, and business processes.

Resources
Economic capacity
(e.g., salaries, equipment,
telephones, purchases) that is
consumed by activities

Work activities
Units of work performed

Final cost object
The ultimate reason for performing
work; the final accumulation
point of cost reassignment
(product, projects, customers)

Performance measures
Measures of how well an
activity meets customer
quality and value and
expectations

Accumulates
process
costs

Process

Reassignment

Segments cost diversity

thinking, it was actually ABC that initially fueled the interest in the early 1980s. (An alternative view reported from the industrial engineering community is that decades ago companies like General Electric were performing cross-functional activity analysis and already using cost data. That use of cost data has progressed into process value analysis, resulting in today's need for permanent, repeatable activity accounting systems.) Regardless of activity accounting's true genesis, it is important to understand the origins of ABC before learning how the data used for product costing also support process and performance improvement.

The major distinction between traditional cost accounting and ABC is that ABC uses non-single-unit production volume cost drivers to trace or reassign activity costs to products or services. In contrast, traditional systems allocate all indirect, variable overhead costs to final cost objects by assuming the overhead's consumption varies at exactly the same rate as a single unit of volume, like a labor hour, a machine hour, an assembled unit of output, or a dollar of purchased material. Allocations assume overhead varies with these factors one-to-one. ABC knows that overhead is more complex, that it doesn't vary with output in that way.

With ABC, an activity cost driver stated in terms of a unit of output (e.g., the number of tools issued from the tool crib to maintenance employees) is used to compute a cost rate for each activity. Subsequently, the activity cost is traced or reassigned to a unique cost object on the basis of how many units of output each activity consumes (or was consumed by) during a defined period.

A misconception about cost drivers has surfaced relating to their role as devices for cost reduction. One hears, "reduce the quantity of the activity cost drivers, and the cost of the activity will be reduced." Be careful. Cost drivers simply explain resource cost consumption. They should not necessarily be the means to reduce costs; cost reduction occurs by altering existing products and processes in response to customers and strategies. Cost drivers are hidden by traditional cost systems, so making them visible via ABC is good; but cost reduction by lowering the incidence of cost drivers may potentially act against strategic intentions or customer needs. Be efficient, but not at the expense of effectiveness.

In summary, ABC can detect proportionate consumption of resources in an organization's interrelated activities; the organization can then reassign the flow of costs into a diverse mix of final cost objects comprised of products, customers, and product sales orders.

3–3. EXPANDING THE CAM-I ABC/ABM CROSS

What matters most is not how the costs flow downward or across through an ABC system but how decision and analysis capability by people is improved. Figure 3–3 expands on the CAM-I cross to emphasize the notion that ABC/ABM data merely serve as a means to an end, with the end being various forms of decisions, assessments, and analysis. The new ABC/ABM data are inert until put to use (i.e., the dashed lines) by decision makers, analysts, managers, or automated instrumentation.

Providing ABC/ABM data to end-users is like turning up the lights in a dark room. It's useful for seeing performance improvement opportunities. ABC/ABM illuminates the content of work in verb-adjective-noun grammar (e.g., "rework defective parts") and presents the costs of business processes across traditional department boundaries. But rearranging the furniture and cleaning house is what ABC/ABM is really all about. That is, ABC/ABM does more than just provide greater visibility and new insights; it enables organizations to make changes. Figure 3–3 expands the CAM-I cross to include the decision-making and diagnostic capabilities that are supported by cost data.

Experienced, successful users of ABC/ABM systems from different companies regularly communicate with each other by phone or at forums to share their applications of the data. Few of these companies are using the data as a tool to control spending. To date, there has been little evidence of after-the-fact spending and variance-to-standard analysis using ABC/ABM information strictly for control purposes. There probably never will be such uses. ABC/ABM is best applied as a forward-looking planning tool, not a historical reporting tool. The most popular uses of ABC/ABM data fall into three broad, overlapping sets of decision and diagnostic capabilities:

1. *Activity-based costing* simply reports what things truly cost without the grotesque distortions from flawed or unnecessary overhead cost practices (i.e., allocations, that dirty word). This new look at old data often brings surprising reversals of what the traditional and misleading accounting system reported as profitable and nonprofitable product and service offerings. Organizations tend to use ABC data more for strategic decisions, like abandoning unprofitable markets or customers, than for tactical decisions. ABC also computes the cost of a process output, for example, the total cost to process an invoice. ABC brings allocation-free, increased accuracy.

Integrated Cost Management

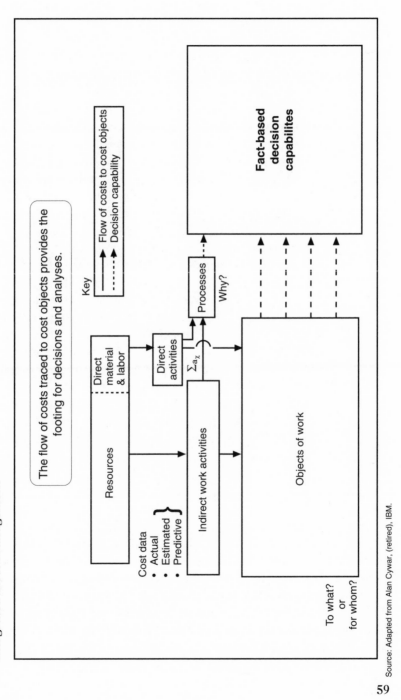

The flow of costs traced to cost objects provides the footing for decisions and analyses.

Fact-based decision capabilites

Key

→ Flow of costs to cost objects
---- Decision capability

Resources

Direct material & labor

Direct activities

Σ_{a_x}

Processes

Why?

Cost data
• Actual
• Estimated
• Predictive

Indirect work activities

Objects of work

To what? or for whom?

Source: Adapted from Alan Cywar, (retired), IBM.

2. *Activity analysis* supports the managerial movement toward continuous improvement and concentrates more on diagnostics and tactical issues. It gives less attention to *what* things costs and more attention to *what causes* or drives costs (i.e., activities)—that is, *why things cost.* Activity analysis and ABM are synonymous.

Activity analysis stems from the new visibility of costs that were hidden in the traditional accounting system. The scoring or grading of activities and processes for their value-content or near-term impactability is a popular extended use of baseline ABM data. Employees can reduce costs by identifying activities that add little or no value. ABM data help prioritize where to alternatively spend problem-solving time and energy for quicker payback. (Activity analysis and ABM are alternatively referred to as process value analysis. They all mean the same thing.)

3. *Forward planning and predictive modeling* is emerging as the most popular application of ABC/ABM data. Once an ABC cost consumption model is completely built, it has been, in one sense, calibrated. It becomes the simulation cost model for the entire enterprise. The model's activity cost driver rates, for example, are reliable for reasonable time periods assuming a relevant range. These rates can be used in conjunction with forecasted quantities of drivers in various scenarios, thus enabling the enterprise to predict future costs. This makes the ABC/ABM data a natural for decisions involving cost-estimating such as order quotations, make-versus-buy analysis, and investment justifications. ABC/ABM is truly a resource consumption modeling tool.

3–4. UNVEILING THE EXPANDED CAM-I CROSS

Figures 3–4 and 3–5 expand on Figure 3–3. Figure 3–4 details the cost objects of work. Figure 3–5 details how each cost object relates to end-user decision-making and diagnostic analysis. As costs incrementally flow from resources through interrelated activities toward the final cost objects of work, more kinds of decision capabilities are enabled.

Prior to tracing activity costs to their final cost objects, an organization can analyze, evaluate, improve, or reengineer processes without knowing precisely what a specific product or service costs. *The focus is on the process.* This partly explains why cycle-time compression and

Expanding the CAM-I Cross

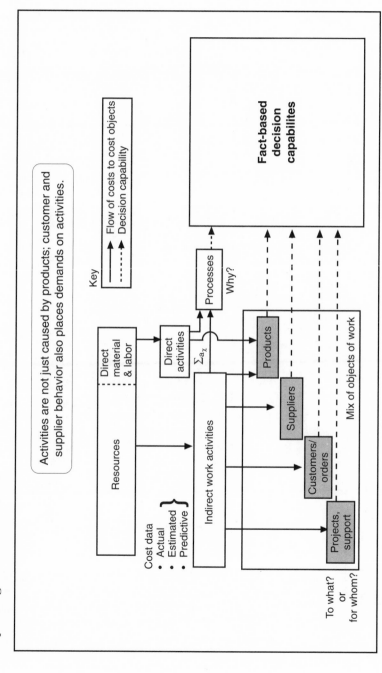

Activities are not just caused by products; customer and supplier behavior also places demands on activities.

Key

→ Flow of costs to cost objects

⇢ Decision capability

Resources

Direct material & labor

Cost data
• Actual
• Estimated
• Predictive

Indirect work activities

Direct activities

Σa_x

Processes

Why?

Products

Suppliers

Customers/ orders

Projects, support

Fact-based decision capabilites

Mix of objects of work

To what? or for whom?

Source: Adapted from Alan Cywar, (retired), IBM.

FIGURE 3–5

Fact-Based Decision Making

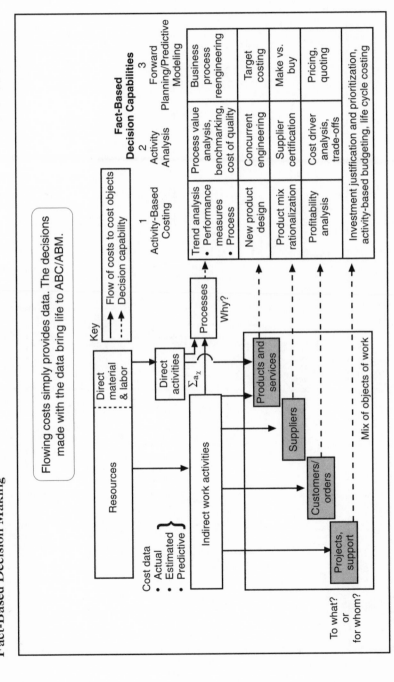

Flowing costs simply provides data. The decisions made with the data bring life to ABC/ABM.

Source: Adapted from Alan Cywar, (retired), IBM.

TQM initiatives are so popular. Their premise is that by improving on time or quality, costs will eventually take care of themselves, somehow exiting the organization. (Of course, ABC/ABM proponents' position is to always consider the impact of time, quality, and cost simultaneously and never to measure or weigh only two of them in isolation of the third.)

The importance of assigning costs to processes prior to embarking on continuous process improvement and total quality management projects cannot be understated. Although these improvement endeavors may appear worthy, without relevant and true cost data, an organization cannot adequately predict the cost impact they may have. Arguably, it may not even easily identify the opportunities for improvement. Finally, the organization cannot easily measure results to demonstrate the solution had an effect.

Here are some basic characteristics about a business process. They should be:

- *Defined* with inputs, outputs, constraints, enablers, and identification of ownership. A customer must exist for the outputs.
- *Controlled* and monitored to detect process variation outside acceptable limits.
- *Effective* in doing the right things.
- *Efficient* in doing those right things well (i.e., don't do the wrong or noncritical things well).
- *Adaptable,* with flexibility to respond quickly to unplanned changes.

Managers and employees are always trying to stabilize processes, but unplanned forces bring imbalances to the business system. Often, reactive expediting and fire fighting can introduce "disturbance activities" that propagate additional unanticipated costs along the business processes.

Next, look at the cost flows being segmented downward in Figure 3–5 into the cost object box. As only the direct and indirect costs that are attributable to producing parts and assembling products are captured, the kinds of decisions that can be made with that cost data tend to be restricted to a product's or service's design and the design process.

Quality function deployment (QFD) is a technique used by development engineers as part of their target costing (refer to Section 1–3C) to rigorously match a customer's requirements to a product's or service's design features. QFD further links these design features to the more critical process characteristics needed to manufacture and assemble the product or deliver the service. This results in concurrent engineering of both product or service design and process design. By managing the process within tolerances, acceptable product tolerances in turn will be assured. QFD forces engineers to make the design more efficient before making the activities more efficient. ABC does not make QFD, target costing, and concurrent engineering happen; it provides cost parameters to simulate varying assumptions about the business and manufacturing processes and to compute trade-offs between features, functions, and costs.

As Figure 3–5's cost object box also shows, some indirect activity costs are strictly attributable to the behavior of external suppliers. For example, some suppliers' product packing and strapping practices complicate the tasks of receiving dock material handlers, while other suppliers' practices do not. The purchased material is not causing the extra cost; it's the external suppliers' behavior. The invoice price from a supplier is therefore not entirely representative of the complete landed product cost to do business with them.

Conversely, some suppliers' capabilities and core competencies make them attractive for organizations to off-load tasks that are currently performed in-house. Twenty-first century ABC/ABM systems will likely expand part-numbering schemes to maintain visibility of the purchased components. These systems may also include the suppliers' part numbers as well, which would be similar to the lot traceability function in government-regulated pharmaceutical and food processing materials management systems software.

Continuing with Figure 3–5 flow of costs, focus again on the cost object box. Some indirect activity costs are strictly attributable to external customer behavior. For example, some customers specify special handling requirements that are outside the norms of the shipping and distribution personnel. In these cases, the finished product or service is not causing any of the extra effort and cost; the customer's behavior is the cause. Imagine that two customers purchase the same mix of items or services from your company, with the same volume, over a year's time. Each of these two customers will rarely consume the same cost. This is because a customer's unique nonproduct-related service needs will place specific demands on your company. In fact, a single customer's service needs may even vary from order to order, irrespective of what products they've purchased from your company.

Tracing the costs that result from specific customer groups, or individual customers, makes sense. After all, customer behavior places demands on the work activities of employees apart from the costs of producing the products or bundling the services. Figure 3–6 below gives examples of profit-friendly and profit-unfriendly customers.

FIGURE 3 – 6

Segmenting Customer Diversity

Profitable and unprofitable customers are distinguished by how they place demands on work activities.

Less Profitable Customers	More Profitable Customers
■ Order small quantities	■ Order large quantities
■ Order special products	■ Order standard products
■ Order low-margin products	■ Order high-margin products
■ Require heavy discounting	■ Require little discounting
■ Make unpredictable demands	■ Make predictable demands
■ Change delivery times	■ Make no changes
■ Require high technical support	■ Require low technical support
■ Pay slowly	■ Pay on time

This behavior can be measured by activity costs and final activity cost drivers.

At this point in tracing the flow of costs using ABC principles to segment diversity, we can conclude that the lowest diversity of activity cost consumption would come from a unique product-customer-order combination, where component parts, ingredients or services are supplier-specific. Twenty-first century cost systems may well flow costs with that much visibility—if it is worth it to decision makers. The amount of detail and accuracy of cost data should be weighed against the risk of not having the data. These trade-offs govern the design of an ABC/ABM system.

Finally, continuing with the cost objects in Figure 3–5, onetime projects and support infrastructure (such as what the accounting function does for a factory, or what a cafeteria does for the accounting function) are facility-sustaining activity costs. Facility-sustaining costs (like contractor lawn maintenance and snow removal services) are defined as those necessary to even be in business, but these costs are not directly caused by customer behavior or products. They have been historically referred to as *fixed costs*. Any attempts to allocate facility-sustaining costs to parts, products, suppliers, or customers is strictly arbitrary. Since these costs are outside the direct control of the process-owners responsible for satisfying product-customer-order combinations, they should be reported separately. The facility-sustaining costs should be isolated but visible, and termed a *surcharge* or an *enterprise tax*. This terminology minimizes any confusion about whether the process-owners or employees can significantly influence infrastructure and discretionary overhead costs that are outside their control.

Figure 3–7 recasts the list of fact-based decision capabilities. It details how tactical or strategic the decisions are and how lasting their impacts might be.

3–5. INDUSTRYWIDE ABC/ABM: EFFICIENT CONSUMER RESPONSE (ECR)

The retail and food industries are recognizing that their suppliers' and customers' behaviors generate a significant amount of their operating costs. These industries have coined the terms *efficient consumer response* (ECR) and *quick response* (QR), supply-chain language that links the total business process from the dirt and raw materials to the end-consumer. Figure 3–8 demonstrates how demands that create work activities are placed on an enterprise.

The key to successfully implementing ECR and QR is recognizing that the customer is truly king or queen and that conflicts between the manufacturers and retailers that precede the customer in the supply chain must be resolved. In most manufacturer-retailer relationships, the two constantly wrestle with each other to gain the next increment of profit. The wrestling introduces extra costs transparent to the end-consumer.

ECR and QR programs dramatically deemphasize the us-versus-them mentality by helping all the companies linked in the supply chain to view themselves a single, unified "virtual" company. As these industrywide participants realize their collaboration produces mutual benefits, they learn to share data and technology, create common standards, and understand each other's cost economics. This enables manufacturers, wholesalers, and retailers to maximize profit along the supply chain.

FIGURE 3–7

Categories of Decisions

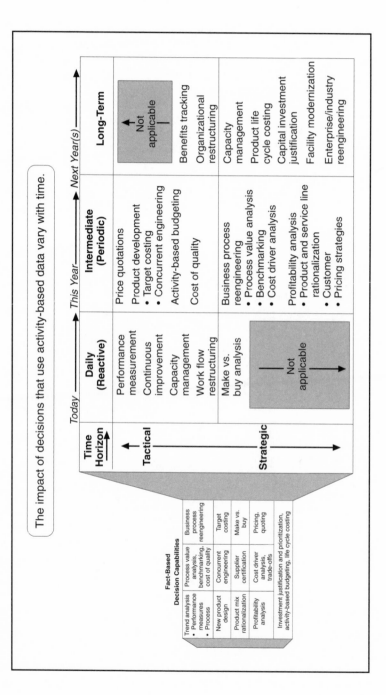

The impact of decisions that use activity-based data vary with time.

67

FIGURE 3-8

The Supplier Value Chain

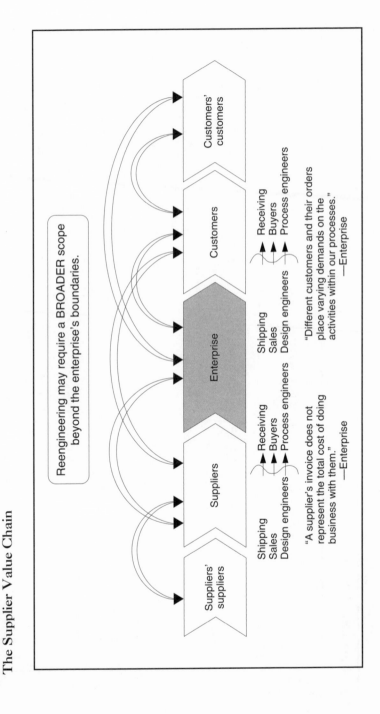

Reengineering may require a BROADER scope beyond the enterprise's boundaries.

Suppliers' suppliers

Suppliers

Shipping
Sales
Design engineers

→ Receiving
→ Buyers
→ Process engineers

"A supplier's invoice does not represent the total cost of doing business with them."
—Enterprise

Enterprise

Customers

Shipping
Sales
Design engineers

→ Receiving
→ Buyers
→ Process engineers

"Different customers and their orders place varying demands on the activities within our processes."
—Enterprise

Customers' customers

The primary enablers for ECR and QR are:

1. Electronic commerce, including electronic data interchange (EDI).

2. Continuous stock replenishment, which links:

   ■ Category management, which monitors point-of-sale data and item shelf-space allocation data.

   ■ Flexible, lean, and agile manufacturing and distribution.

3. Activity-based costing and management.

Figure 3–9 reveals how electronic commerce alone can reduce or eliminate duplication of transaction-related work between two trading partners.

Collaboration among trading partners requires increases in mutual trust, which is obviously lacking given decades of us-versus-them behavior. The use of ABC/ABM data not only replaces intuitions and opinions with facts; it also allows multiple parties to more quickly agree on how they can change their behavior to consequently reduce unnecessary demands for work, thus costs, on each other. Trading partners must tie themselves together.

Beyond collaboration, each trading partner will find greater pressure to unbundle its costs to serve other partners. And each will be rewarded for doing so. There are customer-driven forces for such menu-based pricing; but more important, each partner will have to analyze the trade-offs in decisions about a number of supply-chain issues, ranging from order-size efficiencies and landed-cost pricing to micro-marketing to increasingly segmented customers.

3–6. INTEGRATING PROCESS MANAGEMENT TO FINANCIAL RESULTS

Figure 3–10 is an overarching diagram of the relationships between business processes, decisions, and financial results. In the decisions column appear the costing decisions. To the far right are the economic value added (EVA) financial results. EVA is emerging as the premier measure for monitoring period-to-period creation or destruction of shareholder wealth. It is becoming a popular executive compensation tool because it overcomes some of the flaws of earnings per share (EPS) and return-on-investment (ROI) measures. EVA is also used for allocating capital investments to the highest-yielding opportunities.

70

FIGURE 3–9

Efficient Consumer Response (ECR) Distribution

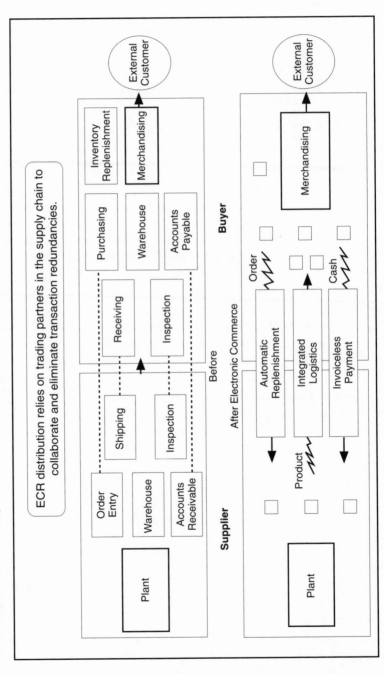

ECR distribution relies on trading partners in the supply chain to collaborate and eliminate transaction redundancies.

FIGURE 3-10

Decisions Produce Results

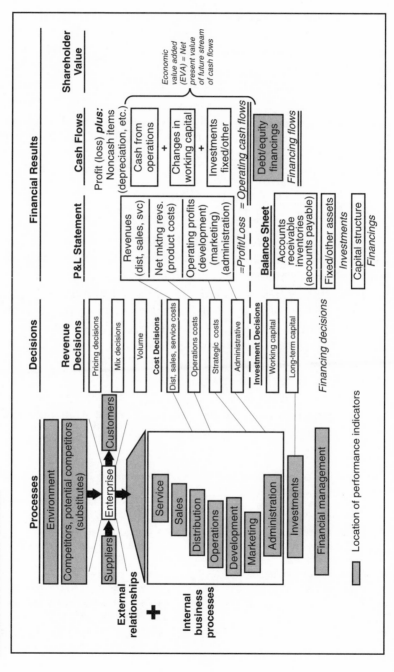

Source: *Developing Comprehensive Performance Indicators*, Exhibit 2, pp. 12–13, The Society of Management Accountants of Canada, 1995.

In Figure 3–11 the cost decisions from Figures 3–5 and 3–7 are appropriately inserted between the processes and the financial results.

There are many management models. Figure 3–12 captures the majority of the elements included in most of these models. ABC/ABM is a measuring system imbedded inside the box labeled "core business processes," but it clearly reaches into the other areas in the diagram.

The next chapter describes techniques to make ABC/ABM measures come alive and "sing" to the those who will use the new cost data to improve performance. These techniques help link the core processes box in Figure 3–12 to the other 10 boxes.

3–7. THE EMERGENCE OF LEAN AND AGILE COMPETITION

The contemporary forces that are leading to more fierce competition have been discussed frequently in speeches and articles: global competition, declining profit margins, customer demands, and so on. Figure 3–13 condenses the migration toward mass customization from an economy initially based on agricultural and natural resources. We are moving toward an Information Age in which large mass-production organizations either collide or collaborate with the niche specialists from the Industrial Age. Alliances of organizations, some for only short terms, are predicted to abound, creating virtual enterprises.

The implications for agile, lean, and virtual organizations with regard to ABC/ABM become evident as we move from Industrial Age structures to Information Age ones:

Industrial Age Organizations	Information Age Organizations
■ Nominal overhead costs relative to direct costs.	■ Sizable overhead support costs of technology dwarfing direct costs.
■ Labor or material volume was acceptable proxy for allocating overhead costs.	■ Traditional overhead allocators are poor and misleading cost drivers.
■ Mass production with standard products.	■ Flexible processes, customized products with information-added services.
■ Focus on efficiency.	■ Focus on value, quality, service, time, and cost.
■ Focus on growth.	■ Focus on being the right size to match customer demand.

FIGURE 3-11

ABC Improves the Cost Decisions

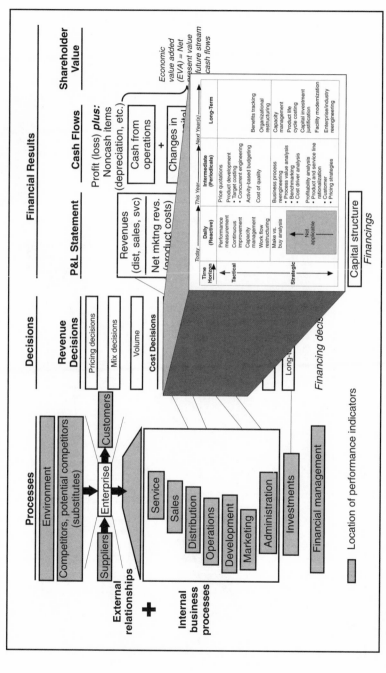

Source: *Developing Comprehensive Performance Indicators*, Exhibit 2, pp. 12–13, The Society of Management Accountants of Canada, 1995.

FIGURE 3-12

Enterprise Business Improvement

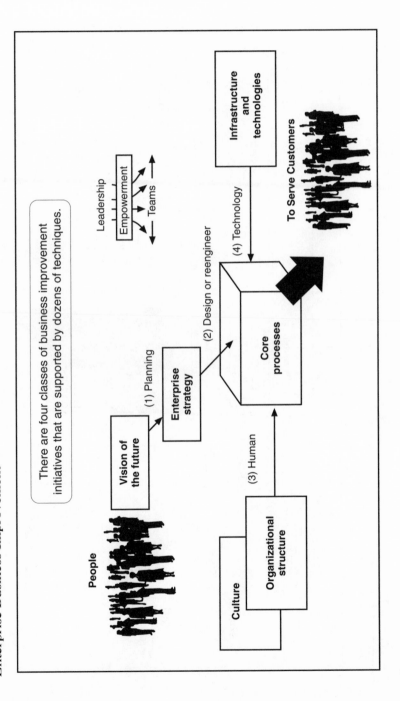

There are four classes of business improvement
initiatives that are supported by dozens of techniques.

People

Vision of
the future

(1) Planning

Enterprise
strategy

(2) Design or reengineer

Core
processes

Leadership

Empowerment

Teams

Infrastructure
and
technologies

(4) Technology

To Serve Customers

(3) Human

Culture

Organizational
structure

FIGURE 3-13

The Emergence of Agility

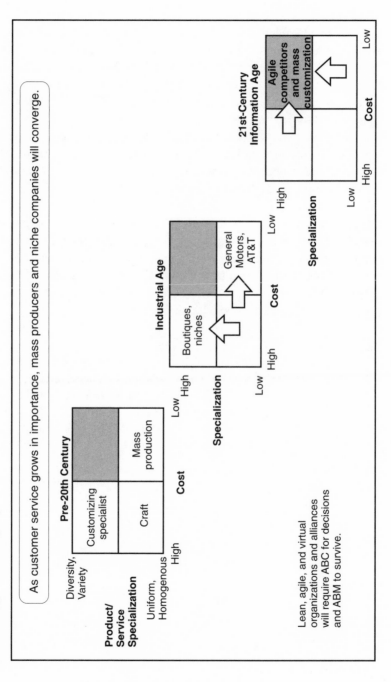

As customer service grows in importance, mass producers and niche companies will converge.

Lean, agile, and virtual organizations and alliances will require ABC for decisions and ABM to survive.

Traditional accounting, a consequence of 19th-century capitalism, satisfies stockholders, bankers, and regulators, not business managers. It is backward-looking and reports data at too aggregated a level in scope and time for managers to use for predictive planning. It doesn't reflect the business process flow very well and is inadequate for tracing shared service costs into the end-products and customer services that are ultimately sold to generate profit.

It is becoming apparent that 21st-century Information Age organizations will leverage collaboration, have flat hierarchies of people, rely on concurrent (not sequential) and parallel from-concept-to-cash processes, and use agile performance measures, often referred to as a balanced score card. It is inconceivable these organizations will be able to make trade-off decisions without ABC/ABM. In the Industrial Age, the customer and financial community were tolerant, lenient, and mostly unknowledgeable of business errors. In the Information Age, the cost of taking risks without gauging the likely consequences will be large. ABC/ABM enhances the kinds of critical decision making that managers and employee teams will be regularly dealing with.

Very often, although a cost system may be nearly perfect and all possible factory economies may have been effected, a manufacturer may nevertheless show losses due to inadequate control over his selling and administrative expenses. In fact, unless the same (costing) principles are applied in controlling selling and administrative costs (as for production), the entire advantage gained through efficient low-cost production may be lost.

William B. Castenholz[2]

---

2. William B. Castenholz, "The Application of Selling and Administrative Expense to Product," *National Association of Cost Accountants (NACH) Yearbook,* 1922.

CHAPTER 4

ABC Is about Flowing Costs

No feature of cost accounting is more difficult than burden distribution. . . . The impression is too widespread that burden is extremely elusive. Cost accountants can do a great deal to counteract this impression by taking advantage of every opportunity to explain the modern methods of distributing burden.

Gould L. Harris[1]

Inexpensive computing and powerful, user-friendly software programs provide greatly expanded capabilities for tracing costs to products using disaggregate cost pools, multiple costing rates, and diverse measures of activity and cost drivers.

H. Thomas Johnson and Robert S. Kaplan[2]

A variety of software vendors have developed computer applications designed for ABC/ABM end-users. Those developments plus fresh thinking about the multiple uses for cost data have raised the level of sophistication for ABC/ABM systems. And being sophisticated does not necessarily equate to being complicated.

All costing techniques involve reassigning costs by flowing or tracing costs from general ledger account balances to someplace else. For example, traditional manufacturing product costing flows an aggregate of overhead cost balances into products using a single cost allocator or driver, usually labor or machine hours. When more accurate product costs were eventually needed, accountants began using multiple cost drivers to reflect the segmentation of diversity and capture proportionate cost consumption of resources by different products or customers. Now that organizations are placing greater attention on managing cross-functional

---

1. Gould L. Harris, "Calculation and Application of Departmental Burden Rates," *National Association of Cost Accountants (NACA) Bulletin,* vol. 1, no. 3, April 1920.
2. H. Thomas Johnson and Robert S. Kaplan, *Relevance Lost: The Rise and Fall of Management Accounting* (Boston, MA: Harvard Business School Press, 1987), p. 224.

business processes, organizations need to expand from two-stage cost flow calculations to ones with multiple-stage cost flows and multiple cost drivers. This better segments the diversity of how activity costs flow into other activities plus gives visibility to underlying processes.

All costs appear in a flow network. Therefore, we will also discuss how to distinguish activity costs by scoring or grading and rationalizing them from a users' perspective. Users need help determining how to act on the data, not just analyzing it.

4–1. TRACING THE FLOW OF COSTS FROM RESOURCES TO FINAL COST OBJECTS

The CAM-I cross in Figure 4–1 presents ABC as a two-stage cost flow technique. Figure 4–2 shows a two-stage multidriver ABC product costing model from the early 1980s. Resources are traced to activities, and activities are traced to outputs.

In the *two-stage ABC approach,* subaccounts of the general ledger are distributed to the various activities in the appropriate proportions using, as they are called in ABC lingo, *first-stage resource cost drivers.* The distributions are based on employee estimates of what activities consume their time and how much. The costs accumulated in these activities are then distributed and reassigned directly to final cost objects using *second-stage activity cost drivers,* such as the number of orders. For example, costs like employee fringe benefits and electrical power might initially be distributed to activities using employee head count and machine hours, respectively, as first-stage resource drivers. Costs accumulated in the various activities are then further traced and reassigned to products using second-stage activity cost drivers such as the number and mix of machine setups, sales orders, purchase orders, machine hours, labor hours, and so forth.

Figure 4–3 shows how an early two-stage ABC model computes activity cost driver rates. Those rates become the basis for reassigning the activity (i.e., verb-adjective-noun) costs to each part, item or service according to its unique consumption pattern. That is, the cost driver unit cost rate is equal to the total activity cost divided by the quantity of activity outputs.

As an improvement to the two-stage ABC approach, the *multiple-stage ABC approach* more closely mirrors the more detailed flow of costs through an organization. Instead of oversimplifying the allocation

FIGURE 4-1

Multiple Cost Views

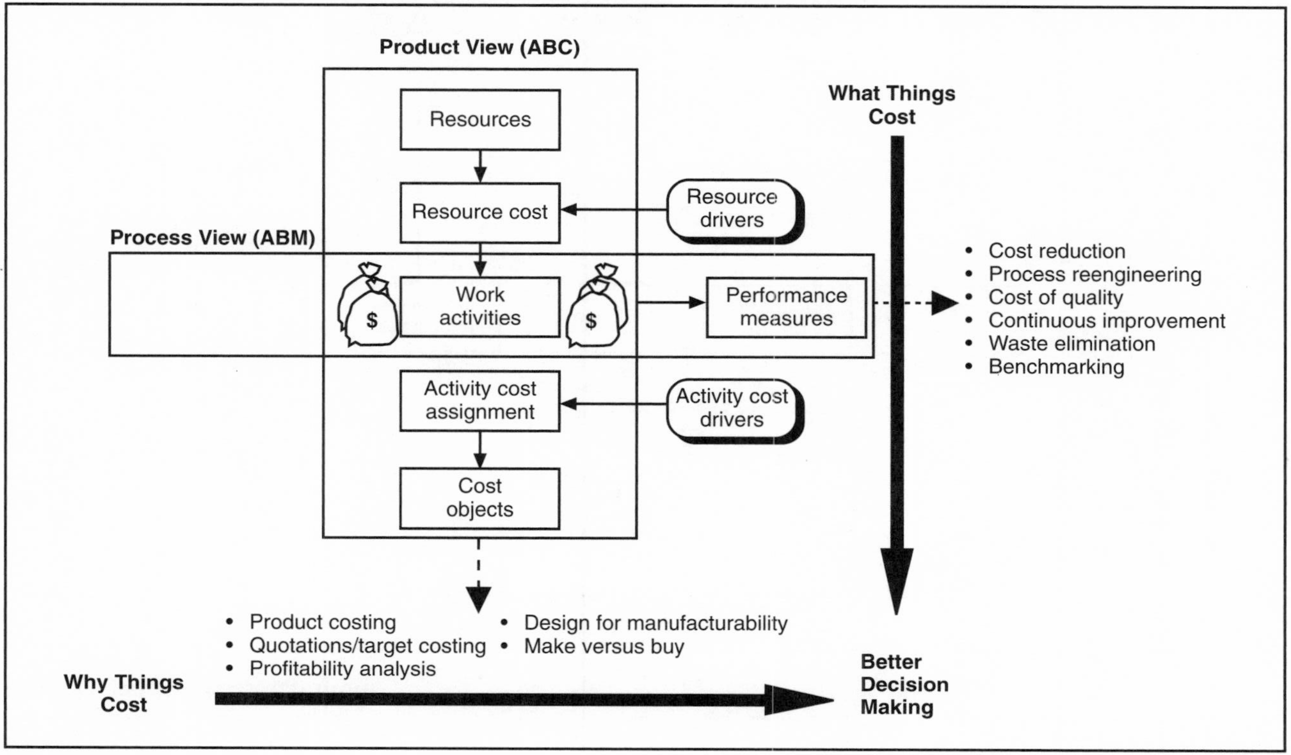

Product View (ABC)

Process View (ABM)

What Things Cost

- Cost reduction
- Process reengineering
- Cost of quality
- Continuous improvement
- Waste elimination
- Benchmarking

Resource drivers

Performance measures

Activity cost drivers

Resources → Resource cost → Work activities

Activity cost assignment → Cost objects

Better Decision Making

- Product costing
- Quotations/target costing
- Profitability analysis
- Design for manufacturability
- Make versus buy

Why Things Cost

FIGURE 4-2

Two-Stage Cost Reassignment

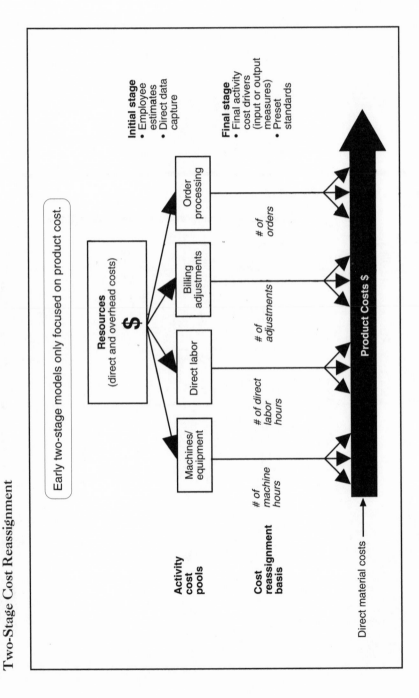

Early two-stage models only focused on product cost.

Resources
(direct and overhead costs)
$

Initial stage
• Employee estimates
• Direct data capture

Final stage
• Final activity cost drivers (input or output measures)
• Preset standards

Activity cost pools

| Machines/ equipment | Direct labor | Billing adjustments | Order processing |

Cost reassignment basis

# of machine hours   *# of direct labor hours*   *# of adjustments*   *# of orders*

Product Costs $

Direct material costs

FIGURE 4-3

Activity Cost Driver Rate Calculation

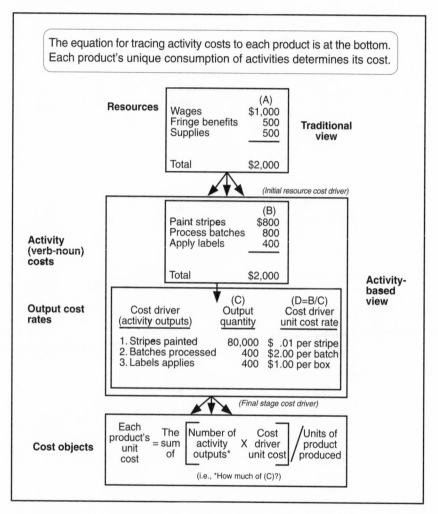

by quickly trying to move costs from their point of incurrence to their final cost objects in just two stages, this approach emphasizes relationships between activities and *other* activities, as well as between activities and their final cost objects. The multi-stage approach recognizes that some activities are consumed by two or more other activities, which in turn are consumed by final products or services.

With multiple stages, and cost assignment drivers, the diversity of consumed resources can be better segmented to truly reflect the costs of product or service proliferation and operational complexity. Refer to Figure 4–4. Following this multiple-stage ABC approach, costs move from initial incurrence to intermediate cost objects in a series of financial tree-branching arterial decomposition steps, all based on cause-and-effect relationships using activity cost drivers.

FIGURE   4 – 4

Multilevel Cost Flowing

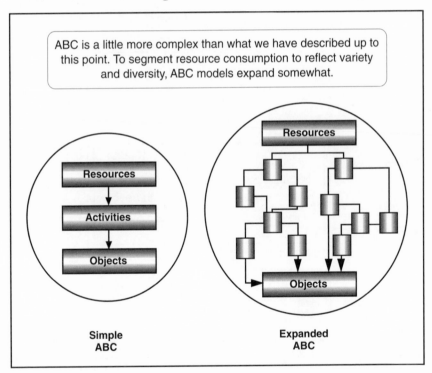

Although the initial assignment of general ledger costs to activities is usually completed using time effort estimates, the subsequent reassignment of the progressively accumulating activity costs to other activities is accomplished using intermediate activity cost drivers. Ultimately, costs are flowed or reassigned to their final cost objects, such as end-products or customers, using final activity cost drivers as in Figure 4–5.

FIGURE 4–5

Activity Data Collection

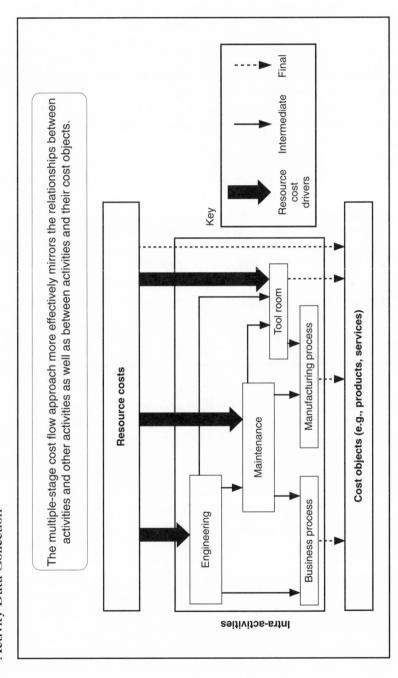

The multiple-stage cost flow approach more effectively mirrors the relationships between activities and other activities as well as between activities and their cost objects.

83

Multiple-stage ABC decomposition is really a series of reassigning costs along flow lines called cost assignment paths. The cost data can be captured both on an incremental (i.e., initial cost driver assignment) and on a cumulative basis (i.e., intermediate cost driver) on its way toward the total cost of the final cost objects. This is an important concept. The initial assignment translates the general ledger account balances into activities. Total costs are reassigned. When the linkages (i.e., cost assignment paths) are networked, end-to-end *cumulative* cost flowing can be accomplished.

Cost drivers serve to reassign costs in realistic proportions to multiple cost objects. In Figure 4–5, note there are three kinds of cost drivers described in place of first-stage and second-stage drivers. There are initial drivers, intermediate drivers, and final activity cost drivers. Figure 4–6 further expands the role of cost drivers. Since a cost flow network is like electric circuitry, with transformer stations, and with dollars replacing the electricity, the different roles and number of stages of the cost drivers do not alter the total dollar amount flowing to the end of the model, but they do give insights as to how they segment diversity of the resources' consumption.

Why have stand-alone computer-based ABC software packages and some integrated business system ABC software modules become increasingly popular since their introduction in the late 1980s? It is because they handle multiple-stage cost flows so well. More so than usually explained in ABC seminars or books, Figure 4–7 displays the complicated cause-and-effect relationships involved in flowing costs from people and equipment (both are resources) through their interrelated activities and into the final cost objects. ABC software is clearly more versatile than spreadsheets, and the ABC models are easier to maintain as changes are made to mirror the business processes.

ABC software can link costs from a node in any stage to one in any other downstream stage—and not necessarily the stage directly below it. That is, costs can skip past stage levels. And the software can track all dollars to be sure that they have been traced and not double-counted or neglected. ABC software effectively reconciles costs traced through the arterial flow paths to the final cost objects. And the software maintains a strong audit-trail memory all the way back to the consumed resources, including staff costs and their activities.

Activity cost flowing has sending and receiving nodes. A sending node of accumulated costs announces, "This is where I am coming

FIGURE 4-6

Cost Drivers Have Different Purposes

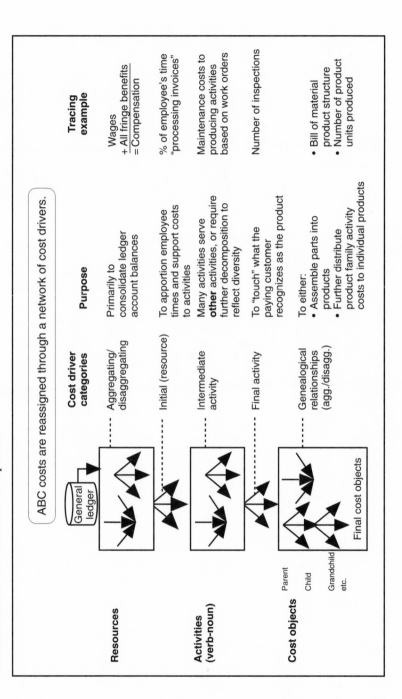

FIGURE 4-7

Arterial Cost Flowing Network

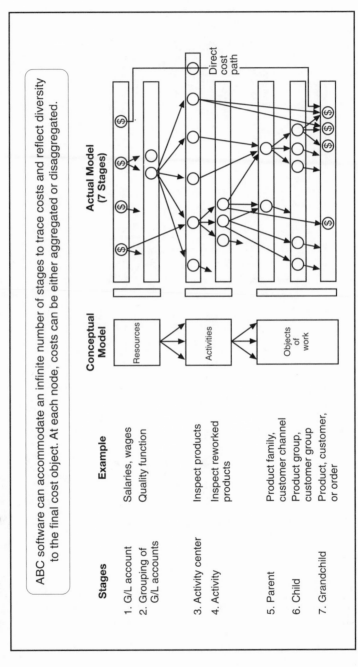

from." The flow lines, which are called *assignment paths,* claim, "This is how much of me." A sending node includes all of the resource and activity costs that precede it. The downstream nodes, which accounting has traditionally called *cost objects,* are targets for which the sending node says, "This is where I am going." The reality is that ABC is a network flow model with arterial traits. It flows costs through nodes. And the flows are in reality reassigning the costs. Figure 4–8 compares ABC with an electrical utility company's flowing of power.

Because of this new and expanded flexibility of arterial network cost flowing, accounting systems are no longer restricted to inflexible level-by-level (department-by-department) step-down allocations favored by traditional cost accountants. And as a bonus, costs can be flowed as work-defining verb-noun descriptions of activities, and not as lump-sums for whole departments. In one sense, flexible ABC cost flowing is to traditional step-down allocations as digital signals are to analog. And everybody is now seeing the digitization revolution with telecommunications, entertainment, and computers.

There is considerable confusion with cost flowing. A two-stage ABC model with multiple final activity cost drivers will compute substantially more accurate costs of cost objects than a model with a single type of final activity cost driver. If that's your only goal, then use a spreadsheet. But ABC computations will "hit the wall" on a spreadsheet if you want end-users to physically relate to intra-activity behavior. The practical limits of a spreadsheet approach are not easily stretched. The view provided by multiple stages, linked by intermediate activity cost drivers, will more logically and closely resemble a process diagram more than a functional organization chart.

A helpful mental model of the multiple-stage cost flow is to consider lots of people waiting for elevators at the top floor of a multistory building. Assume there are an ever-increasing number of elevators as the floors descend; this represents the ability to segment diversity. Each person (i.e., a resource cost) can exit at any floor and switch to another downward elevator to potentially repeat his or her exit-and-entry path. Or they can directly continue on to a lower floor or to the bottom, first floor (i.e., to the final cost objects). This last route would imply a more dedicated resource serving a special product family or customer group. Eventually all the people get off on that first floor, but the elevator door from which they exit and the unique indirect path they take dictates the unique cost, reflecting diversity through segmentation.

FIGURE 4-8

What Is ABC?

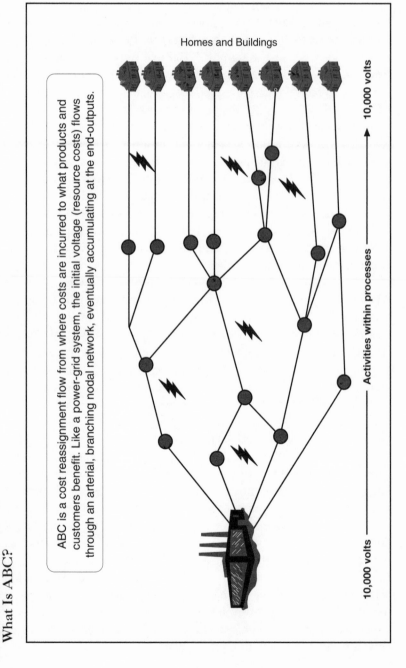

Homes and Buildings

ABC is a cost reassignment flow from where costs are incurred to what products and customers benefit. Like a power-grid system, the initial voltage (resource costs) flows through an arterial, branching nodal network, eventually accumulating at the end-outputs.

10,000 volts

Activities within processes

10,000 volts

Figures 4–9 through 4–13 are five progressive graphics that demonstrate activity cost decomposition. Note how the resource cost drivers initially translate 100 percent of the costs; then the intermediate and final cost drivers link the relationships.

Figure 4–13 proves the conservation of total cost theorem, that is, with ABC, no costs can be created or destroyed. (You probably remember a similar theorem from high school chemistry about the conservation of total energy.) ABC flows the initial $70 of expenses from the profit-and-loss statement into the final cost objects, consisting of customer products and services.

In the overly simplistic two-stage cost allocation model diagrammed in Figure 3–3, resources are consumed by activities and those activities in turn are consumed by final cost objects. In reality, the multi-stage model is a cascading waterfall of cost flows traversing through a network. Some costs flow directly to a final cost object, for example, a special employee assigned and fully dedicated to a single product for a single particular customer. Other costs flow indirectly from resources through a multitude of cost accumulating collection points (which are intermediate cost objects) eventually downward into specific final cost objects. The lowest or most detailed final cost object is a specific product-customer-order combination. Through each path, the cascading cost flows are effectively reassigning costs and reporting visibility of as much cost diversity as economically possible. A well-designed ABC model is the ultimate in segmenting costs to reflect diversity, variety, and uniqueness. Repeating the analogy, ABC is to traditional step-down allocations as digital is to analog.

One of the more confusing aspects of designing ABC models is differentiating the levels of detail and the degrees of granularity. It is helpful to think of levels of detail applying to activities and degrees of granularity applying to final cost objects. Figure 4–14 contrasts the financial decomposition of cost flowing to final cost objects with financial sequencing to accumulate the end-to-end costs of the process.

The cost of work activities are the pivot or intersection between the vertical (decomposition) and horizontal (accumulating) views. The greater the decomposition, the more granular the final cost objects. In contrast, the greater the level of detail of work activities, the more the verb-adjective noun activities are divided into their work tasks. The former addresses the cost of things sold whereas the latter quantifies how and why they cost what they do.

FIGURE 4-9

Direct Costs to Products and Support Departments

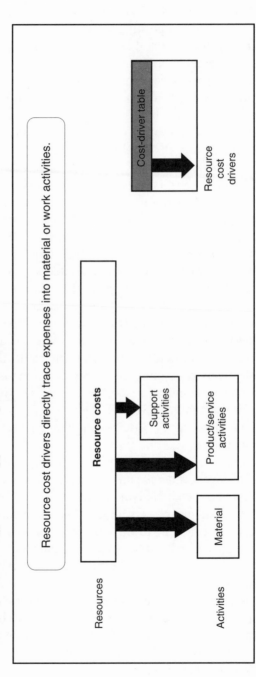

Direct Costs to Customers and the Infrastructure

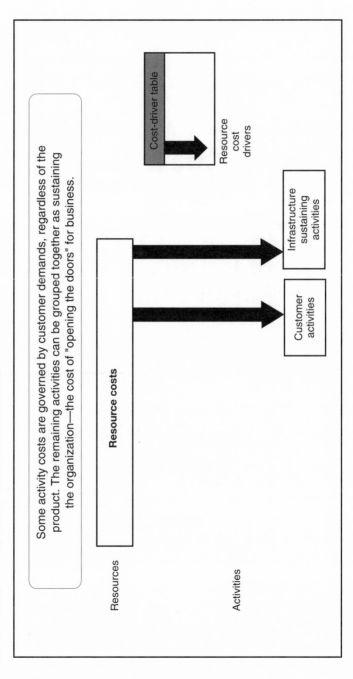

FIGURE 4-11

Tracing Product Costs to Customers

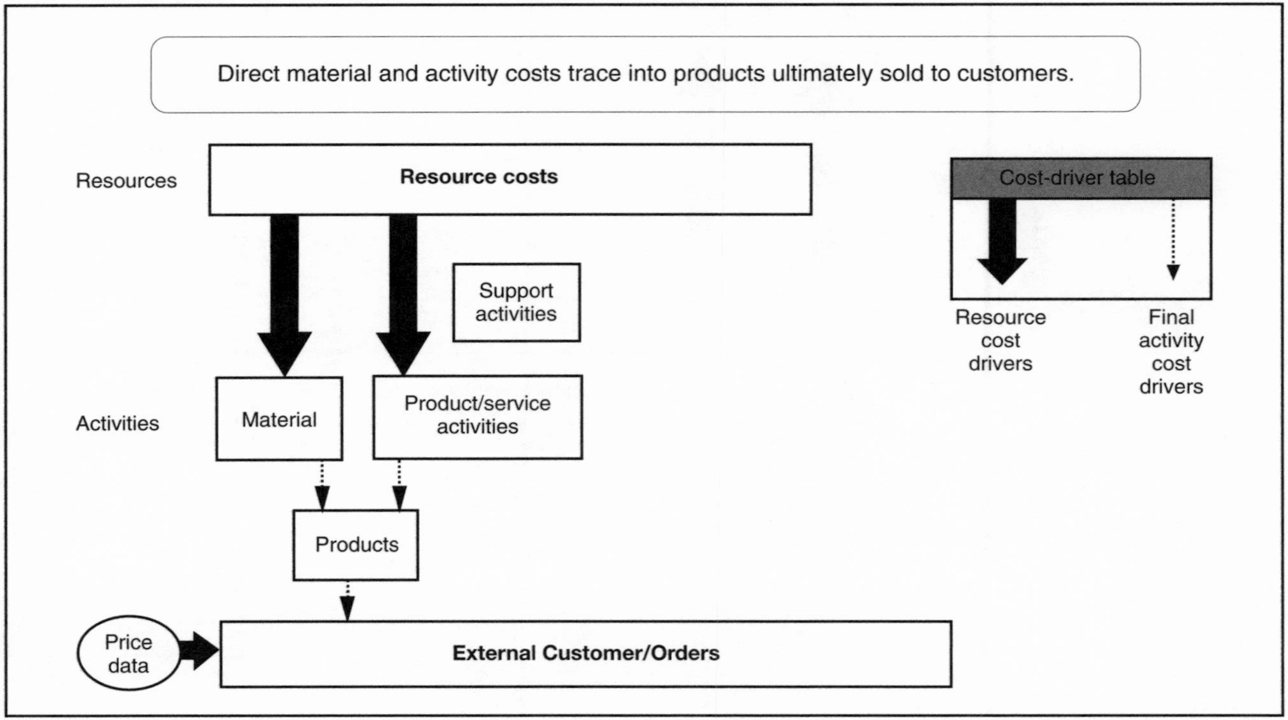

Direct material and activity costs trace into products ultimately sold to customers.

FIGURE 4–12

Tracing Intermediate Costs to Customers

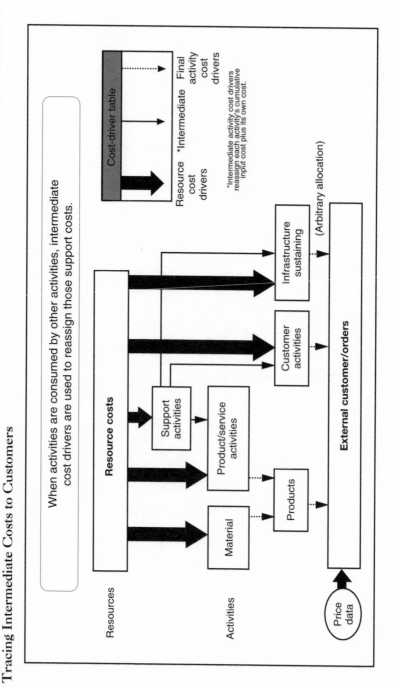

FIGURE 4-13

Reassigning Resource Costs to Cost Objects

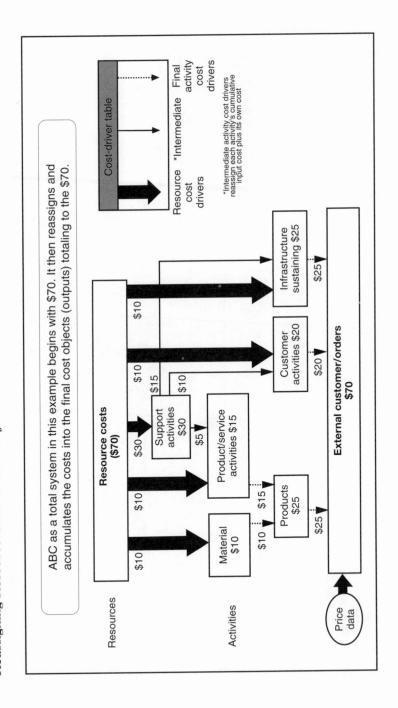

FIGURE   4 – 1 4

Decomposing versus Accumulating Activity Costs

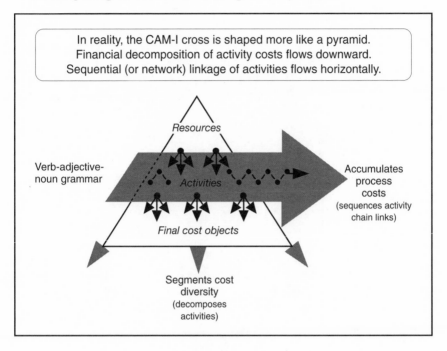

In reality, the CAM-I cross is shaped more like a pyramid.
Financial decomposition of activity costs flows downward.
Sequential (or network) linkage of activities flows horizontally.

Resources

Verb-adjective-
noun grammar

Activities

Accumulates
process
costs
(sequences activity
chain links)

Final cost objects

Segments cost
diversity
(decomposes
activities)

4–2. THE EVOLUTION OF OVERHEAD COST SYSTEMS

In an ideal world, all resource costs could be directly charged or assigned from a people or machine resource to a specific product or service customer. But in our practical world, there is so much complexity and technology that most resource costs are initially incurred in the form of indirect overhead. From a historical perspective, cost accountants accepted this and summarized or grouped indirect resource costs into pools before introducing those costs into their traditional cost flowing systems.

Figure 4–15 shows a five-step evolutionary path of cost accounting practices designed to reassign overhead costs to final cost objects.

The first two generations or approaches represent traditional cost accounting systems with whole departments' costs uniformly allocated,

FIGURE 4-15

Evolution of Overhead Cost Allocation Practices

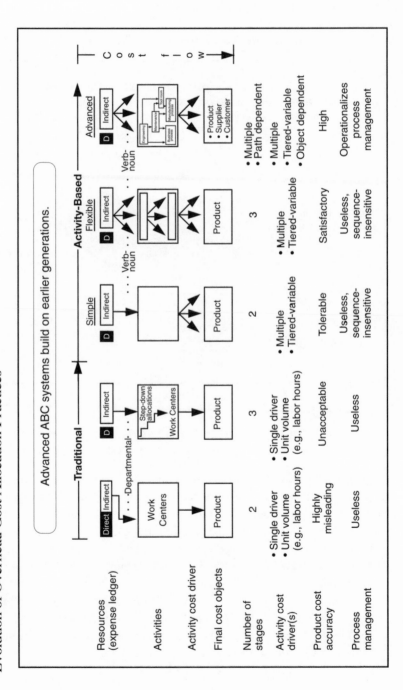

usually using arbitrary and inappropriate factors like square feet or head count. The last three generations are increasingly activity-based and grow in progressiveness from left to right.

The *simple* ABC approach uses activity cost drivers that are not tied to units of volume input/output, such as labor hours, sales dollars, or completed products or services. This approach subdivides whole departments of people by using action verb-adjective-noun descriptions of activities. But in the simple approach, the work described as activities is not related or sequenced end-to-end. The approach only segments the diversity of resource consumption by activities.

The *flexible* ABC approach begins adding more stages of cost redistributions to give more freedom to segment cost diversity. As a result, product, service, or customer related costs can be computed more accurately. But as in the simple approach, the individual activities remain insensitive to their sequencial relationship in an end-to-end process. This ABC model does not need to know, nor care, how activities relate to each other within a business process. It primarily aims to financially decompose activity costs with little regard to operational uses of the data.

The *advanced* ABC approach incorporates process-based thinking. The activities are now linked end-to-end as a process chain network or weblike artery system. This advanced approach usually has well over three stages of cost redistributions to segment diversity, variety, and uniqueness. The cost assignment paths will more closely mirror the business process flowchart, and employees in operations will recognize this distinction compared to the earlier generations.

The process flow network can decompose work activities to lower levels of detailed work tasks while the costing of segmented diversity can remain at a higher level (you may wish to peek at Figure 7–26). Depending on where the activity cost driver is attached to its final cost objects, all of the resource costs flow (with an understanding of why they flow) to reach a product or customer.

Advanced ABC better facilitates process-based management. This is the direction the cost management revolution is headed. Activity related information is used to manage the activities performed and understand their causes in order to reduce the costs consumed by those activities. Improved and more accurate product or customer costing is a natural by-product of the process cost model.

4–3. COST PUSH VERSUS DEMAND PULL ABC SYSTEMS

ABC software vendors initially chose one of two methods to calculate and reassign costs: (1) activity-based cost decomposition or (2) customer consumption demand. Both methods trace and reassign 100 percent of an organization's costs. Their differences are in the direction they trace the costs. The former pushes costs from resources to cost objects, while the latter goes in the reverse direction.

Sections 4–1 and 4–2 described activity-based cost decomposition. The emphasis is on segmenting diversity of resources and their activity costs to more accurately reassign these costs into products, services, and customers.

The alternative ABC calculation method starts with the cost objects and, working in the opposite direction, asks which primary activities are consumed and how much. Customer demand is the driving force. Support or secondary activities are similarly consumed by the primary activities. The activities are viewed as consuming the resource costs of payroll and purchased items or services. This method results in ABC cost flow designs that more physically mirror the business process flow work steps as compared to the activity cost decomposition method. By declaring standard activity cost driver rates, this method allows isolating excess capacity costs for each activity. Managing capacity to meet dynamic demand loads is becoming popular for all operating managers.

At the risk of confusing the reader, Figure 4–16 asks if the process flow approach is superior to the activity cost decomposition approach. The answer depends on the intended purpose of the cost data, but both approaches can be designed to calculate the exact same costs of the final cost objects.

It is easier to achieve accurate cost object costs through the activity cost decomposition approach because its cost flow network is unconstrained by requirements to chronologically link activities to other activities. In contrast, the process flow approach mirrors the physical reality of how work gets done, which appeals to those focusing on the costs of the process. However, the process flow demand pull approach can concurrently trace and keep track of the various diversities through the network. In the end, the total costs reassigned by each approach must be equal, and both approaches can be designed such that those totals are also equal for each final cost object.

FIGURE 4-16

Two Alternative ABC System Designs

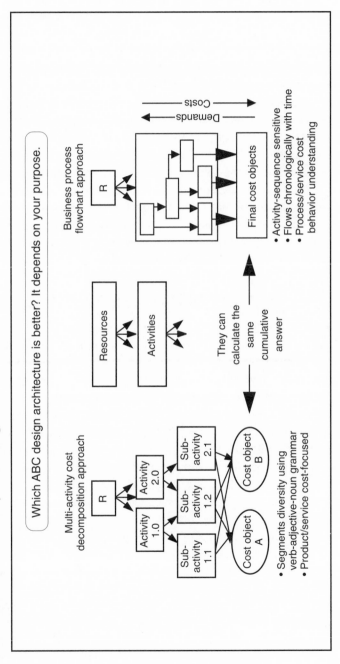

99

The CAM-I cross has served an important purpose: educating people on how resource costs can be translated via work activities into a product view and a process view (see Figure 3–1). However, the CAM-I cross can also send a confusing message that the two cost views might be independent or not connected. In reality, the product and process views in the cross converge to meet at the same point. The cross should be shaped like a wishbone, with the far right end of the horizontal (processes) view bent downward to touch the bottom end of the vertical (product, or final cost objects) view bending to the right. At the touchpoint, the cumulative resource costs have been totally reassigned.

Let's return to the subject of ABC software vendors. They all appreciate that end-users desire what-if simulations of scenarios to predict costs or to identify future capacity constraints. Figure 4–17 shows an example of using cost estimating to quote a price for a customer order.

ABC software vendors are converging toward functionality that combines cost push and demand pull logic.

4–4. ELEMENTS OF RESOURCE COSTS

An important step in developing the ABC system's cost flow is to initially organize its elements of resource cost into two categories: material costs and activity costs.

Consider material costs to be all nonpayroll costs representing purchases that are moderately related and conveniently traceable to a specific product or service. Most of these types of cost, like raw materials, are obvious and have traditionally been treated as direct costs.

Activity costs are the people and equipment-based conversion costs involved in performing or supporting the activities that take place within the organization. These costs would include all labor and fringe benefit costs, as well as other closely associated "super-fringe benefit" costs, like laptop computers or phone bills, normally treated as overhead in a traditional cost accounting system. For key equipment activities, the costs include amortized depreciation. Refer to Figure 4–18.

Material costs can be traced directly to the products or services whose throughput measures drive the costs. For example, the raw materials, purchased components, and some outside contractor services that go into a manufactured product are all driven by the units of throughput of that particular part. An example would be a hospital's purchase costs for each x-ray that requires the same variety and size of film. Two other

Demand Pull Cost Estimating

After an ABC model is calibrated, with cost driver rates, the demands placed on work activities derived from a new customer order can be accurately costed for a profitable quote.

101

F I G U R E   4 – 1 8

Two Categories of Resource Costs

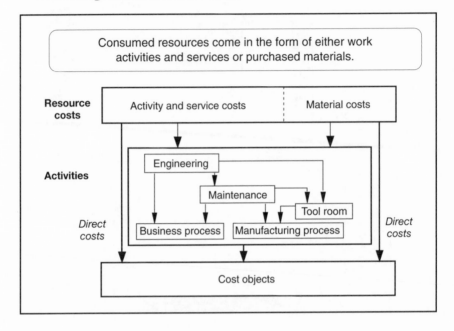

examples would be the purchase costs for each instant oil change in a maintenance garage for a particular type of automobile that requires the same amount of oil, or for each unit of particular size and variety of consumer product that requires the same packaging when shipped to a retailer. Organizations refer to these measures as material standards.

Activity costs, on the other hand, are people- and machine-related and are traced to the activities whose drivers make the costs necessary. Indirect material and supplies as well as other contractor services can be traced to intra-activities where they eventually get traced to final cost objects. Once accumulated in the activities, the cost of each activity is traced to each product or service, or to another activity whose drivers make the activity necessary. Indirect material, supplies, and contractor services are hitching a ride with the work-activity costs along the cost flow pathways.

4–5. USEFULNESS OF INDENTED CODE– NUMBERING SCHEMES

Indented code-numbering schemes allow displaying the subtotals of a total. Subtotals can be repeatedly nested below the total they make up.

Indented coding schemes simplify the flowing of costs by allowing a downward decomposition of activity costs and dividing wholes into their pieces, as shown by Figure 4–19. The same indented coding schemes also allow upward summarization and cost roll-ups to higher aggregates. Remember that the most detailed data will always be captured at the lowest level verb-adjective-noun code for an activity, and every cost reported above it must be a sum total created by formula or equation.

One's initial impression of subdividing activities with indented code-numbering is in the direction of levelness—activities are broken into tasks. But there is also a direction of diversity caused by the cost object driver. The same activity can be divided by what or whom it serves to improve granularity. The factors influencing the ABC model design will always swing between a process view and a product view.

Remember that the financial decomposition of activities reassigns costs, whereas the accumulation of end-to-end activity costs within a business process (at some level) is additive.

Business processes were previously defined as a sequence or network of activities, regardless of the activities' level of detail. By decomposing functional areas into large numbers of activities for the purpose of segmenting diversity, the activities can be recombined to understand costs across the core business processes. For example, a business can determine all of the costs involved in the process used to procure needed raw materials, purchased components, indirect materials, and outside processing services. First, the functional areas such as purchasing, material handling, shipping, receiving, inspection, accounts payable, and quality control are decomposed into verb-adjective-noun activities that describe employee efforts (e.g., process purchase order) in the procurement process. Then, only those activities from each functional area that apply can be recombined into the process to arrive at the desired cost information. This is an electronic way to "string the pearls."

To make it easy to convert an activity from its functional role to its process role, simply assign the same activity two code numbers, one by function and one by process. Then roll up and report the newly assembled costs by process.

FIGURE 4-19

Indented Cost Roll-Ups

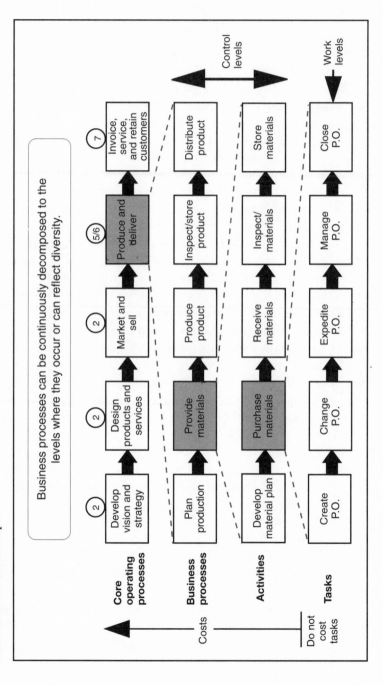

Business processes can be continuously decomposed to the levels where they occur or can reflect diversity.

4–6. SCORING ACTIVITIES TO FACILITATE MANAGERIAL ANALYSIS AND ACTIONS

When the total ABC/ABM model has been completed to the point where all resource costs have been entirely flowed via activities into final cost objects, the dollars will have then been appropriately segmented to reflect diversity. But this dollarized information alone does not necessarily convey to anybody what to do or how to improve. The dollars have not been differentiated from each other except in their relative magnitudes. The activity dollars need to be further differentiated into user-defined categories to facilitate managerial analysis. Without differentiation, the activities will all look the same except for their description and dollar amount.

Organizations interested in performance improvement can use grading methods to evaluate the activities that contribute to the output of goods or services according to whether or not the activities are necessary, support critical strategic success factors, or are performed efficiently. Various coding methods are used for this scoring of activities; these range from the very simple value-added/non-value-added approach to differentiating methods using very complex criteria. The idea is to eliminate non-value-adding activities and optimize value-adding activities, thus enabling employees to focus on the worth of work. Employees can see how work really serves customers and which activities are wasteful. Focus and visibility are enhanced because people can more easily see where costs are big or small and what costs can be impacted or managed in the near term. Scoring costs invokes action beyond just gazing at and analyzing costs.

The most popular differentiating categories are often called activity metrics or attributes and they are "attached" to the activity costs. They are presented in Figure 4–20:

- Impactability or urgency.
- Value-added content.
- Effectiveness in performing the activity.
- Importance in supporting management's strategic plans.
- Quality (i.e., conformance) content.
- Cost influencing content.

FIGURE 4-20

Examples of Scoring Attributes to Influence Actions

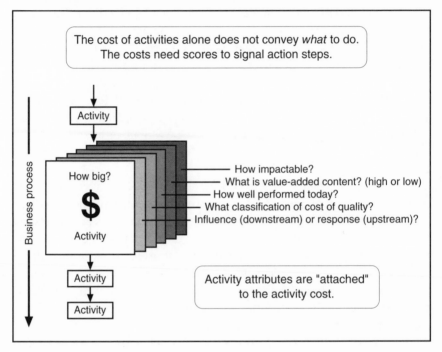

In addition to categories, there are multiple views from which to grade activities:

- From a customer's or process owner's view.
- From the product or service's view.
- From the enterprise strategy's view.
- From an efficiency view.

Collectively, these views can provide trade-offs for what-if cost analysis.

Employee teams usually customize their own approach by differentiating categories from multiple views and defining the scoring scale for each specific category using complex criteria. The underlying principle is that activities can be scored or graded at the lowest activity level, like a gene in a chromosome, which then allows the scored cost to uniquely accumulate into any cost roll-up or cost recombination involving two or more activities. Insights are gained as the marked activity dollars are combined, and then analysis can show both where and how intense problems or opportunities might be. This new visibility of cost assists end-users to focus and reach consensus.

Scoring can be done "blindfolded"—that is, by first objectively assessing the activity independent of the amount of the costs it consumes, which will vary over time with improvement. The employees who score or grade can be a different team than the employees or functional representatives who defined the activities and estimated the costs.

Why are the categories just mentioned popular? How are they used to move employees and managers from performing analyses to taking actions?

- *Degree of impactability or urgency.* Each lowest-level activity can be graded for its near-term and long-term impactability as high, medium, low, or none. Alternatively, a percent of impactability can be estimated for each activity to test and quantify the aggregate cost savings opportunity that currently is based on gut feeling or a nonquantitative, nondollarized judging scheme. Employees usually score an activity's impactability high if they believe it is non-value-adding. As an option, activities can also be graded by the necessity to change their consumption level in order to align activities with strategic goals or to remove waste.
- *Value-added content.* This scoring scheme has evolved over time. This evolution has moved from a focus on the dichotomy of either value-added or non-value-added, to the degree of value-added (e.g., high, medium, low, none), to value-creating from a customer's view, value-enabling from a product's or a process' view, non-value-adding from all three of those views, and the degree of value added.
- *Effectiveness level.* This scoring scheme assesses how well the performance meets the activity or process customer's expectations (e.g., exceeds, meets, below).
- *Importance level.* This scoring scheme relates each activity to how well it supports management's strategic goals (e.g., critical, essential, necessary, postponable). A test question for each activity is, "If we stopped this completely, what would be the consequences?"
- *Quality content.* This scoring scheme, shown in Figure 4–21, classifies each activity and supports the popular TQM categories

FIGURE 4–21

Cost of Quality Using Activities

Companies can assign activity attributes to cost of quality (COQ) categories.

	Conformance		Nonconformance	
	I Prevention	II Appraisal	III Internal failure	IV External failure
Definitions	Activities designed to prevent errors and mistakes during make and delivery	Activities to review, audit, evaluate, or measure to assure conformance	Activities correcting errors **prior** to customer receipt	Activities correcting errors **after** customer receipt
Activity group examples	• Training • Advanced quality planning • Perform SPC • Fool proofing	• Incoming inspection • Editors' review • Line inspection • Approvals • Finished goods inspection	• Process scrap • Rework • Unplanned downtime	• Handle complaints • Warranty charges • Process returns • Expedited late order • Lawsuits

Take actions to shift costs to lower overall COQ

as follows: cost of conformance (prevention activities and appraisal and test activities), and cost of nonconformance (internal failure activities and external failure activities).

- *Cost influencing content.* This scoring scheme attaches and associates a specific upstream activity with a specific downstream activity that was caused upstream. There is an effect-based relationship between activities. An example is a less preferable or short-changed engineering design activity that later results in an undesirable engineering change activity.

In summary, the scoring of activities brings colors and shadings to the ABC/ABM model; without such scoring, all dollars are devoid of any nonmonetary value. By differentiating dollar cost with scoring and grading schemes, the managerial analysis is greatly improved and the attention and focus of employees can be better directed.

Figures 4–22 through 4–28 show how three separate scoring schemes can be combined to determine what actions to take. The dollar amounts are communicated by the size of the circles. The three scores are for:

- Degree of value (horizontal axis).
- Degree of effectiveness (vertical axis).
- Degree of support of critical success factors (shaded quartiles of the circles).

FIGURE 4-22

Four Quadrants to Directionally Suggest Actions

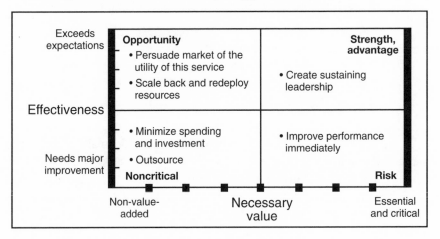

The first two scoring scales combine to form two axes, which in turn create four quadrants. Each quadrant uniquely indicates what possible actions can be taken.

Figure 4–23 shows how the three scoring variables (value, effectiveness, critical success factor impact) and the cost magnitude variable can be simultaneously combined.

F I G U R E   4 – 2 3

Four Variables

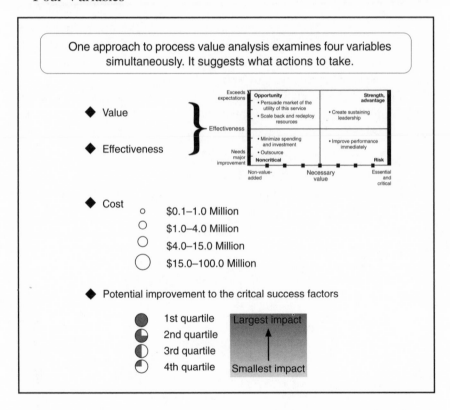

Figure 4–24 shows an example of why it would make sense for a large dollar activity located in the lower right-hand "risk" quadrant to be targeted for increased investment and improvement.

Figures 4–25 through 4–28 present examples of activities and business processes for each of the four quadrants. This graphical technique

FIGURE 4-24

Attributes Suggest Taking Actions

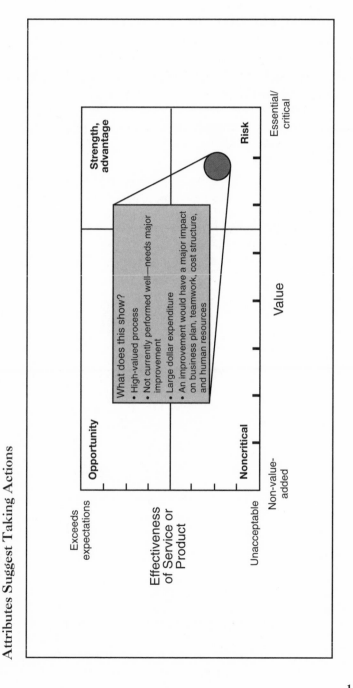

works best when comparing many different and somewhat unrelated activities. An example would be when evaluating headquarter operations where many business processes are isolated and self-contained. In contrast, for examining core business processes containing many activities, use the diagramming techniques in Figures 7–22 and 7–25.

Generally speaking, managers tend to be risk adverse; they overanalyze and underexecute. There is a paralysis to take action. Using these diagramming techniques and those in Chapter 7 will directionally suggest to managers what to do.

> It may be well to state at the outset that a satisfactory cost system must be built *up* from the factory, not *down* from the accounts; the problem must be approached primarily from a . . . production and not from an accounting point of view.
>
> *H. G. Crockett*[3]

---

3. H. G. Crockett, "Some Problems in the Actual Installation of Cost Systems," *National Association of Cost Accountants (NACA) Bulletin,* vol. 1, no. 8, February 1921.

FIGURE 4-25

Noncritical Activities

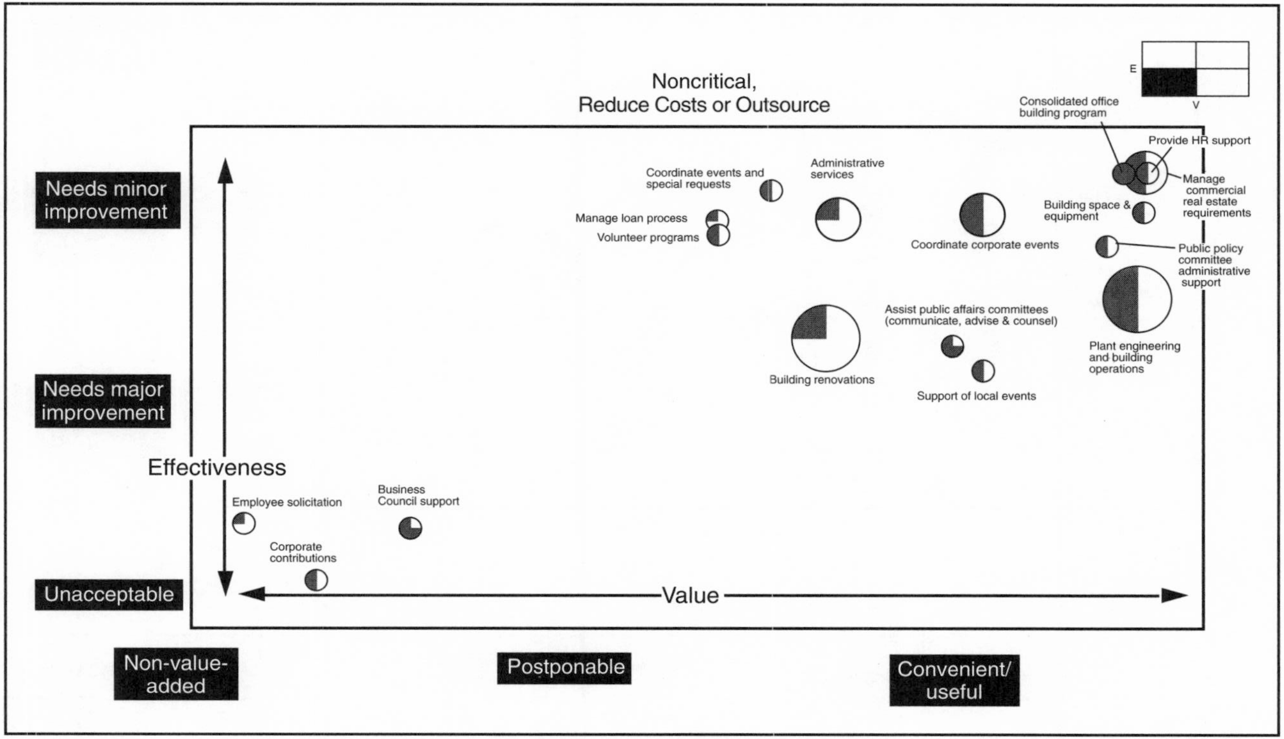

114

FIGURE 4-26

Risk Activities

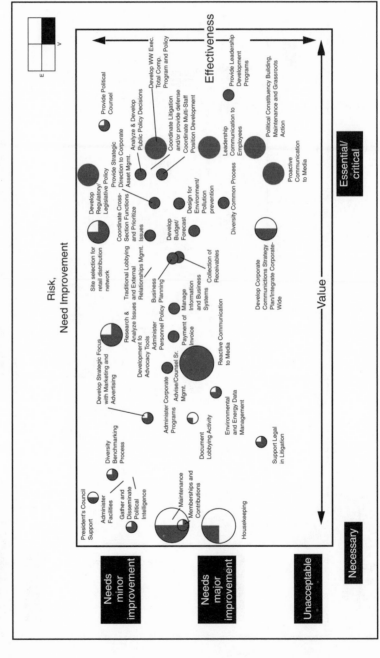

FIGURE 4-27

Potential Opportunity Activities

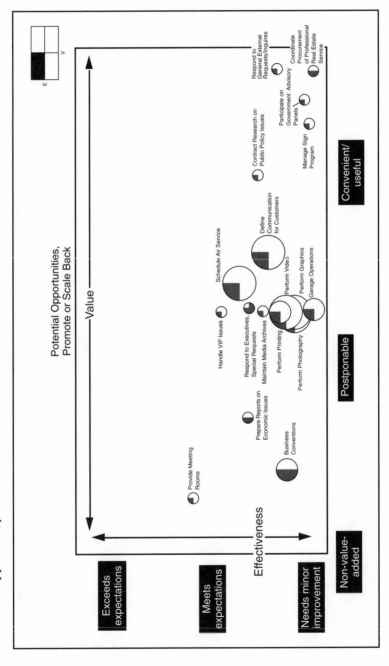

FIGURE 4-28

Leverage Activities for Advantage

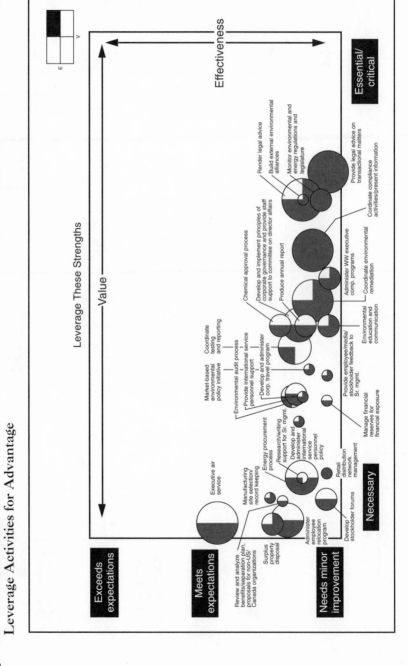

CHAPTER 5

The Unification of Time, Cost, and Quality

No facts that are in themselves complex can be represented in fewer elements than they naturally possess. While it is not denied that many exceedingly complex methods are in use that yield no good results, it must still be recognized that there is a minimum of possible simplicity that cannot be reduced without destroying the value of the whole fabric. The snare of the "simple system" is responsible for more inefficiency and less than is generally recognized. . . .

Alexander H. Church[1]

The choice of management accounting systems is as closely related to the behavioral sciences as it is to economics and the decision sciences.

Charles T. Horngren[2]

5-1. FAILED PROMISES FROM TQM AND JIT MANAGEMENT

Today's business managers are recognizing how systemically connected quality, time, and cost really are. Point solutions are being exposed as ineffective. In this new era of permanent "everyday low prices," a company must simultaneously achieve better, faster, and cheaper to retain customers and attract new prospects. Focusing only on time and quality, and excluding the cost dimension, exposes a company to potentially spending inordinate amounts of time and money in remote parts of the business without improving the bottom line impact. For example, project managers often break capacity bottlenecks with costly investments only to find a more constraining bottleneck downstream, thus negating any bottom line impact from the earlier spending.

---

1. Alexander H. Church, "Organisation by Production Factors," *Engineering Magazine,* April 1910, p. 80.
2. Charles T. Horngren, *Cost Accounting: A Managerial Emphasis* (Englewood Cliffs, NJ: Prentice Hall, 1977), p. 172.s

In problem solving today, it is getting more difficult to simply focus on a specific. One needs to focus on where the process leads to the specific. In effect quality, time, and cost are derivatives of the process. And depending on what you fix or change, there may be a high correlation with cost or time or quality. In the end, we are the sum total of all the things we do.

One of the premises of TQM and JIT is that organizations carry excess and unused capacity in workers. Therefore, by reducing error and waste, less people will be required to achieve the same (or greater) output. Removing the waste will reduce the cost and make the unused capacity more available to manage. In the 1990s, organizations are experiencing problems with these improvement techniques, and consequently time-compression and TQM programs are losing some of the popularity they enjoyed in the 1970s and 1980s (Figure 5–1).

There is a paradox here. The TQM initiatives that companies pursue and the day-by-day tactical decisions they make all feel like winners. But surprisingly little of the investment and spending show up on the bottom-line! What is going on here?

Here's the situation. Both time reduction and quality improvement programs involve team approaches to solutions that are predicated upon employee empowerment and involvement. Employees get very excited and feel good with their new liberation and begin suggesting and creating ever-increasing numbers of small projects. In time, too many projects to properly manage arise, and in many cases, the employees lose respect for their management's ability to deal with it all. This can eventually backfire on management in two ways. If management is unresponsive, the employees question management's commitment and credibility. Alternatively, by giving project teams license to pursue suggested initiatives, management may be suboptimizing funding and efforts, with teams bumping into walls and colliding with each others' suggestions. Funded initiatives often shift work and costs upstream or downstream, but not out of the enterprise. The costs behave like water inside a squishy water balloon. Press here and costs show up there. The cost savings consequently never show up on the bottom line. Refer to Figure 5–2.

What is the problem? For starters, at many companies the low-hanging fruit has frequently already been picked. Furthermore, some fairly indiscriminate across-the-board employee terminations may have already been mandated. Meanwhile, the cycle-time reduction and TQM project teams are all being encouraged to challenge the beliefs about

FIGURE 5-1

Cost Measures Are the Missing Link

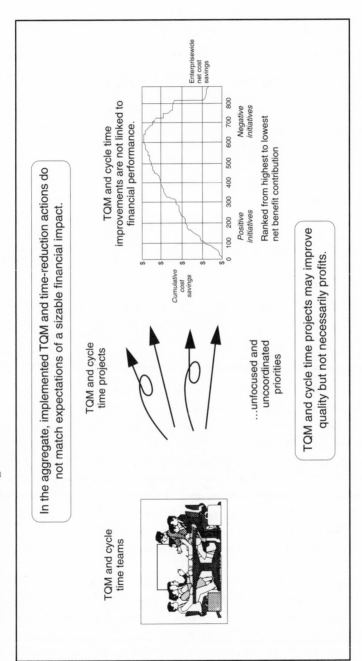

In the aggregate, implemented TQM and time-reduction actions do not match expectations of a sizable financial impact.

TQM and cycle time improvements are not linked to financial performance.

Enterprisewide net cost savings

Cumulative cost savings

Positive initiatives

Negative initiatives

Ranked from highest to lowest net benefit contribution

TQM and cycle time projects

...unfocused and uncoordinated priorities

TQM and cycle time teams

TQM and cycle time projects may improve quality but not necessarily profits.

F I G U R E   5 – 2

Department versus Department

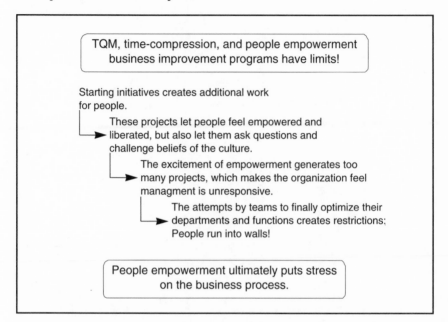

their business, customers, and customs; and they are boldly surfacing up invalid or out-of-date assumptions and sacred cows about their enterprise and their culture. As they do, conflicts arise at the business process level, not at the task or procedure level. For example, a procurement improvement team may want its material managers and suppliers to behave in a manner quite different from that being recommended by a separate material receiving improvement team. In short, the empowerment of employees is in reality bringing stress upon out-of-date and potentially dysfunctional business processes, as shown in Figure 5–3.

This is not a minor problem. Some people have referred to management's fondness for TQM and JIT as a "ceremonial rain dance around the campfire." Just send all your employees to quality and cycle-time management training school because it looks and feels good. What will correct this manage-by-feel approach? One solution is the increasing emphasis on customer satisfaction.

Attention to a customer's needs and wants is increasing dramatically. This growing awareness is today driving many business improvement

FIGURE 5-3

Finding the Real Problem

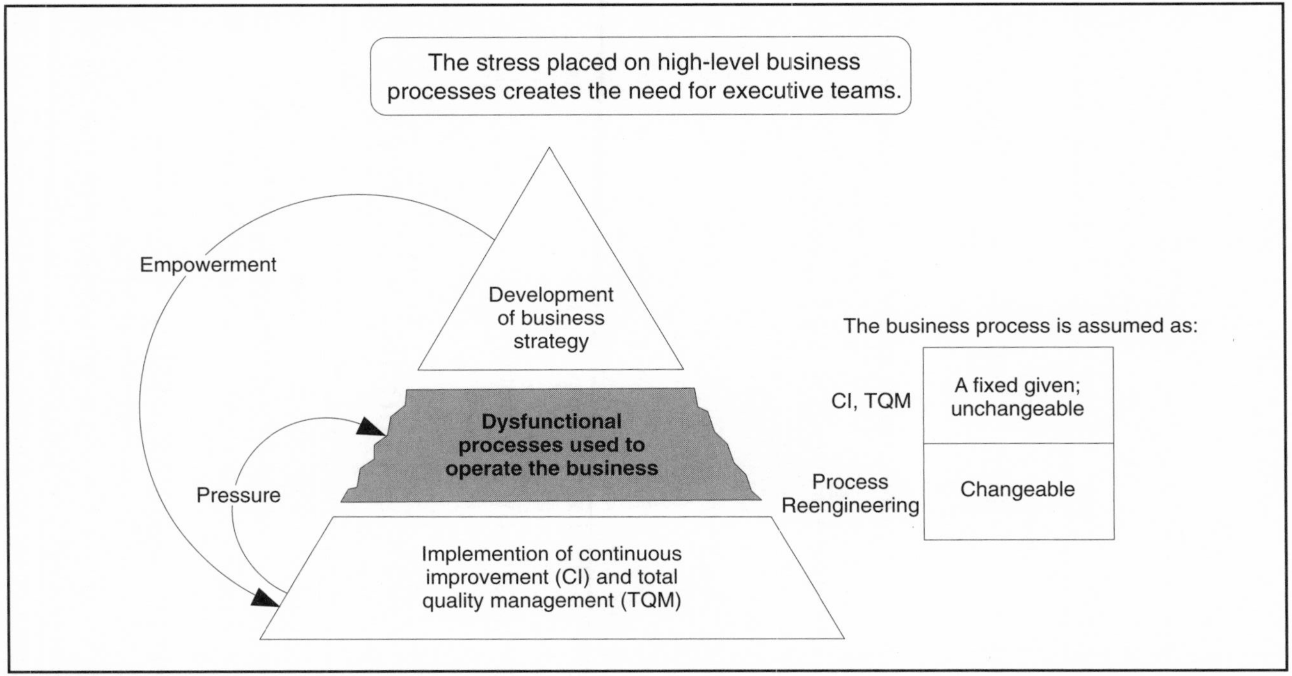

The stress placed on high-level business processes creates the need for executive teams.

Development of business strategy

Dysfunctional processes used to operate the business

Implemention of continuous improvement (CI) and total quality management (TQM)

Empowerment

Pressure

The business process is assumed as:

| CI, TQM | A fixed given; unchangeable |
| Process Reengineering | Changeable |

programs, such as business process reengineering. Companies now recognize that customer requirements are forever expanding and are unbounded. A one-size-fits-all attitude toward customers, a legacy of the Henry Ford Model-T mass production era, is being replaced by a highly flexible delivery system to accommodate the customers' growing appetite for variety, diversity, and immediate delivery. Economy of scale loses its importance under these conditions of mass customization and defers to agility.

Understanding cost behavior will become increasingly important for managers and teams of all levels to assess the trade-offs between costs and benefits in all forms of business decisions. Figure 5–4 portrays how companies are achieving command over an increasing number of capabilities. Because these capabilities are systemically and holistically interconnected, activity-based accounting principles are playing a critical role in helping managers and teams test, gauge, and quantify the future impact of planned changes on the enterprise's costs.

Understanding how an organization collectively behaves as a whole becomes important as complexity increases because cause and effect become more separated in both time and location.

What is needed as a solution are executive improvement teams comprised of senior level managers whose view is at the higher cross-departmental business process level. Time-reduction and TQM projects need to be linked further to financial performance, and only activity accounting can accomplish that feat.

5–2. ABC VERSUS THEORY OF CONSTRAINTS VERSUS THROUGHPUT ACCOUNTING

In the early 1980s, a physicist specializing in fluid dynamics named Eliyahu M. Goldratt captivated operations managers' attention with his Theory of Constraints (TOC), an approach to material flow control based on bottleneck properties. He mesmerized people not only with the simplicity of the theory's approach but also by describing major flaws in traditional full-absorption accounting.

First, the flaws. Goldratt started his speeches with, "Cost accounting—enemy number one of productivity!" He would then describe how the accountants' cost allocation practice of applying overhead costs to products on the basis of labor hours or machine hours (or any unit-based input/output factor) is also used to measure a work center's utilization

FIGURE 5 - 4

Shift from Products to Processes

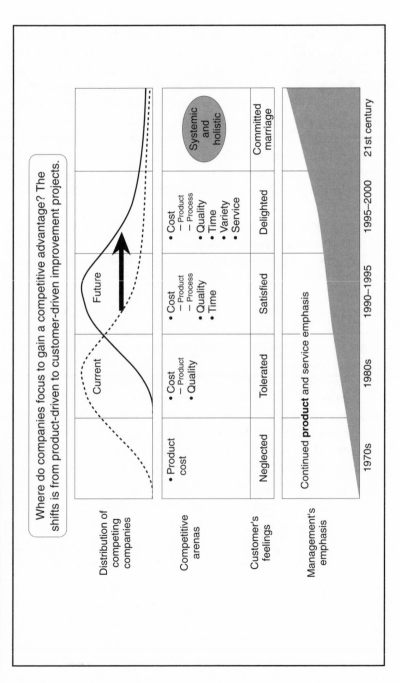

Where do companies focus to gain a competitive advantage? The shifts is from product-driven to customer-driven improvement projects.

	1970s	1980s	1990–1995	1995–2000	21st century
Distribution of competing companies		Current	Future		
Competitive arenas	• Product cost	• Cost – Product • Quality	• Cost – Product – Process • Quality • Time	• Cost – Product – Process • Quality • Time • Variety • Service	Systemic and holistic
Customer's feelings	Neglected	Tolerated	Satisfied	Delighted	Committed marriage
Management's emphasis	Continued **product** and service emphasis				

and efficiency performance. Measuring the productivity of a work center without regard to the *total* system inadvertently motivates behavior that, while individually appearing good, collectively is contrary to just-in-time managerial thinking and adversely affects the total organization's efforts.

For example, an unintended outcome of giving workers incentives to report a maximum number of hours or units of output at their workstations is that the total system fills up with lots of intermediate, unassembled, or unfinished components without regard to the "right" products or services at the "right" time and place. Goldratt was correct. He knew from his physics training that one must take a total systems view when there are work-flow interdependencies and limited resources or capacity for production. Consequently, he recognized that a single bottleneck or capacity constraint would effectively govern the total output of an entire facility. One of Goldratt's mantras is, "Manage the flow, not just the capacity." By using better scheduling of piecework production, a system can actually get relatively more total output than with the traditional approach of always adding overtime or buying extra equipment or workers. In effect, the net total cost of this haphazard and continuous practice of constantly adding capacity at local workstations actually exceeds the cost of just better scheduling the flow of items to be worked on through the existing capacity.

This leads to another one of Goldratt's mantras: "The sum of the local optimums will never exceed the global optimum." So in conjunction with explaining what is bad about traditional cost accounting, Goldratt also provided a vision of what a better replacement cost system would look like. Having both a criticism and a solution is a basic formula for overcoming organizational resistance to change. His replacement costing approach is simple and very appealing to logic:

- You start with basic assumption that the goal of any profit-making business is to make money.
- The replacement cost accounting then falls neatly into place by focusing on the three possible dimensions of money:
  1. Throughout (T)—the rate at which the system (i.e., the business) generates money through sales.
  2. Inventory (I)—all the money the system invests in purchasing things it intends to sell (i.e., direct and associated indirect materials).

3. Operating expense (OE)—all the money the system spends
in converting inventory into throughput (e.g., wages, fringe
benefits, depreciation, capital charges, subcontracted labor, or
support costs).

Throughput costs effectively become the total sales less purchased direct
material. Inventory costs are not comparable to the financial accountant's
goal of constantly attaching on-the-fly expenses for point-in-time valuation of work-in-progress or finished goods inventories. Theory of Constraint (TOC) cost accounting obviously adapts a different view that disregards interim valuation of inventory (see Figure 5–5).

This new view of costs brings greater emphasis to material flow velocity and has spawned the name *throughput accounting*. It recognizes
that capacity constraints are gating factors to making profit and that any
time lost at a bottleneck is forever lost to the total business and results in
lost profit (conversely any time gained from removing a nonbottleneck is
a mirage with no bottom-line impact despite the extra effort).

From here things get sticky. TOC advocates assume that much or
all of the overhead cost allocations can be loaded at the bottlenecked
work center. This escalates the cost of any part, product, or service that
uses that work center, which conversely reduces loaded costs to similar
items going through nonbottlenecked work centers. The resulting calculations yield dramatically different product costs and clearly penalize
items "renting time" at the bottleneck. The new cost measures are used to
understand directionally where incremental product profit may come
from and to aid future planning for capital or resource spending.

Here is one of the rubs. TOC advocates criticize ABC data because
it can produce different cost numbers than theirs. Since throughput accounting supports JIT thinking and all of the TQM-related philosophies
that go with JIT, to TOC advocates ABC data appear both wrong and bad.

In practice, most operating environments are well balanced with
regard to production rates and available capacities; and managers are
getting increasingly better at flexibly moving people and reprioritizing
schedules. Most companies are moving toward scheduling and dispatch-
ing near-term planning systems that include finite (as opposed to infinite) forward capacity logic with much broader views and more frequent
schedule refreshing than in the past. These things are what industrial and
process engineers are paid to do. The net effect is that operations are
fairly well balanced; any significant imbalances, which create the

FIGURE 5-5

ABC versus Theory of Constraints (TOC)

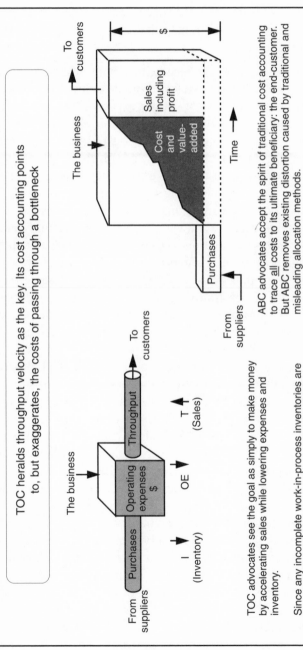

TOC heralds throughput velocity as the key. Its cost accounting points to, but exaggerates, the costs of passing through a bottleneck

TOC advocates see the goal as simply to make money by accelerating sales while lowering expenses and inventory.

Since any incomplete work-in-process inventories are a derivative of the product delivery schedule (assuming available capacity always exists), TOC disregards the traditional accounting practice of "valuing the inventory," which does not serve TOC's purpose.

ABC advocates accept the spirit of traditional cost accounting to trace all costs to its ultimate beneficiary: the end-customer. But ABC removes existing distortion caused by traditional and misleading allocation methods.

ABC advocates disclose insightful information about all work centers, what drives them and what will be the enterprisewide impacts of changing them.

bottlenecks, usually come from the demand schedule of different orders with different due dates. The implication is that the bottleneck wanders— and it wanders a lot. Like soap bubbles bursting, the bottleneck is here, it's there, now it's over there.

TOC advocates like throughput accounting because it removes the adverse effects of overhead absorption practices that give workers incentives to locally optimize their personal performance, thus glutting the system with ill-timed buffer inventories and all the baggage of waste, obsolescence risk, exposure to defects, and so on. Even more appealing, throughput accounting draws attention, using the organization's financial system, to the TOC advocates' political concerns about where the next and precious scarce dollars should be spent.

But wandering bottlenecks create a need to constantly recalculate where the loaded costs will shift. This also yields a yo-yo effect on product costs, which can be disturbing to sales and marketing personnel, who have financial rewards tied to profit margins that are shifting with the bottlenecks. Figure 5–6 diagrams a comparison of ABC and TOC.

ABC data is not volatile. It does not concentrate on the direct costs, which vary with a high correlation with the output of primary parts, products, outputs, and services. What ABC does do is concentrate on the costs of all of the other indirect work activities. ABC acts as a proxy for a direct costing system by linking the activity costs that support the end-products and services, which appear to many people as fixed costs. ABC accomplishes this by flowing costs through an arterial assignment network of cause-and-effect drivers. Therefore, ABC more accurately captures product costs, which will vary only to the degree that the quantities of their cost drivers vary—and the majority of those costs have little or nothing to do with the bottleneck or where the bottleneck is located at any moment in time.

TOC advocates find great appeal in accelerating the pipeline's velocity. By putting the measurement spotlight on the pipeline, the organization will directionally know where to spend its incremental dollars. In addition, throughput accounting removes accountability from all the support costs, which usually include the costs of the TOC advocates themselves. TOC advocates excuse themselves from measurement in the belief that by reducing cycle time and synchronously taking buffer inventory or work out of the system, they have decreased overall costs, automatically taking care of the costs for their services. Well, maybe.

FIGURE 5-6

ABC versus Theory of Constraints (TOC)

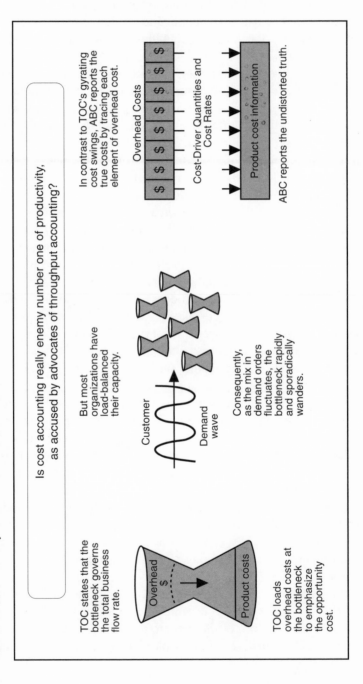

Is cost accounting really enemy number one of productivity, as accused by advocates of throughput accounting?

TOC states that the bottleneck governs the total business flow rate.

Overhead $

Product costs

TOC loads overhead costs at the bottleneck to emphasize the opportunity cost.

But most organizations have load-balanced their capacity.

Customer

Demand wave

Consequently, as the mix in demand orders fluctuates, the bottleneck rapidly and sporadically wanders.

In contrast to TOC's gyrating cost swings, ABC reports the true costs by tracing each element of overhead cost.

Overhead Costs

$ $ $ $ $ $ $ $

Cost-Driver Quantities and Cost Rates

Product cost information

ABC reports the undistorted truth.

ABC produces distortion-free visibility to costs, cost behavior, and cost accumulation. It provides a foundation from which better decisions can be made, such as for marginal costing or incremental volume cost justifications. The ABC foundation is a solid web of cause-and-effect relationships. ABC costs do not gyrate; they rise and fall to the waves of customer order demand and to quantity changes of the activity cost drivers. In the end, ABC is simply a mirror in which the organization can examine its cost economics, particularly its increasingly swelling indirect costs.

The time horizon is actually what seems to divide TOC and ABC advocates. For example, the TOC camp would claim that the cost of a shortage from a missing 50-cent bolt is worth 100 dollars of premium airfreight, not 50 cents, if its shortage will delay shipment of a $100,000 order. The cost depends on other circumstances. Just as in physics, when the speed of mass approaches the speed of light, traditional (Newtonian) rules give way to bizarre ones (Einsteinian physics). But in practice, few things we know move at the speed of light, so we can apply traditional equations of physics. Similarly, few resource costs in an enterprise are affected by a bottleneck or near-deadline delivery date. ABC reports actual costs of resource consumption, assuming normal operating conditions that reflect expediting and reacting behavior. In contrast, TOC overstates costs and points to problems that may in fact only be temporary.

In sum, ABC works well for costs that occur away from bottlenecks and for costs of those activities not associated with completing late or potentially late shipments or services, usually a wild period.

Although they recognize that ABC calculations do not yet dynamically mirror the operations environment, ABC supporters would like to think that operations planners can master the tasks of scheduling and loading work centers according to changing demand orders. ABC supporters will work toward a cost system that will benefit all end-users.

5–3. ABC AND UNUSED CAPACITY MANAGEMENT

In defense of ABC, there is a movement to report the costs of unused capacity to a relevant level of detail. With more relevant data, it is hoped that the organization will behave directionally toward the aspiration that Goldratt pronounced: to make money. There will forever be natural tension between sales and production. ABC data can be reformatted to remove much of that conflict and to introduce a neutral target for both sales and operations to attack for their mutual benefit. The neutral target for both groups to focus on is costly unused capacity.

Sales can remove unused capacity by filling it with orders. Operations can remove unused capacity by streamlining, by removing capacity-consuming yield losses, and by better scheduling the product or service flow.

This ABC movement starts with the premise that true total capacity should be measured 24 hours a day, seven days a week, for an entire year. This is technically referred to as theoretical capacity. Within this truly total capacity, one can begin to measure theoretical capacity's elements as either containing:

1. Idle capacity—no use for reasons of policy, union rules, legal regulations, holidays, or simply insufficient sales demand (the last item is a key reason).

2. Nonproductive capacity—time where resources are either being held for an expected workload; being used to produce what will subsequently be discovered as scrap loss or rework; being repaired, serviced, maintained, or trained; or being set up and changed over to produce the next scheduled product or service.

3. Productive capacity—time used to actually work on what the customer is buying or to practice on or break in new products or new processes.

When capacity is segmented this way—at a fairly granular level, such as by each producing work center—both sales and operations personnel can focus on a mutual enemy: nonproductive capacity. Operations people can focus on removing it with faster setups and higher equipment uptime, resulting in an increase in idle capacity, which in turn provides an opportunity to fill more sales orders. Salespeople can remove nonproductive capacity by adding more sales orders, which also increases productive capacity (see Figure 5–7).

This new focus on unused capacity leads to an obvious question: Which part of the nonproductive capacity do you focus on? It depends on how much nonproductive capacity exists and where. In most organizations there is little or no relevant data. You cannot manage or communicate well without accumulating data. You cannot measure what you do not define. You cannot define what you do not understand. So you first better understand what you are even trying to manage.

FIGURE 5-7

ABC and Unused Capacity Management

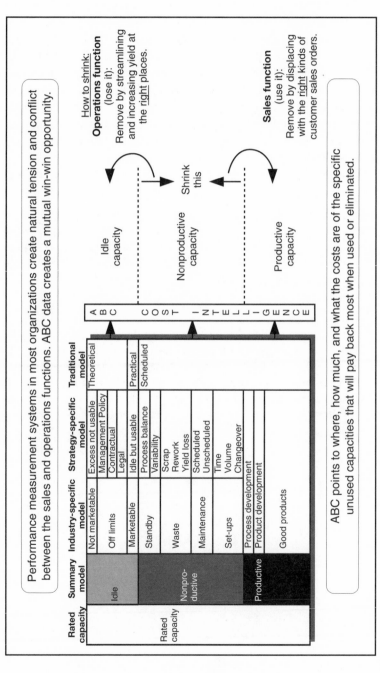

Performance measurement systems in most organizations create natural tension and conflict between the sales and operations functions. ABC data creates a mutual win-win opportunity.

ABC points to where, how much, and what the costs are of the specific unused capacities that will pay back most when used or eliminated.

Source: Consortium for Advanced Manufacturers–International (CAM–I), Cost Management Systems (CMS) Program, 1995.

131

In attempting to understand unused capacity, ABC advocates have determined that managers can segment total theoretical capacity into the three classes above (with further segmentation within each) and measure ABC cost data at individual work centers to that same level of granularity. And it can even differentiate sunk costs (e.g., depreciation) from controllable expenses (e.g., a laborer's time) to the same level of detail.

The benefit is that nonproductive unused capacity can be measured enterprisewide and quantified as cost. Both sales and operations managers can then focus on problem areas, assess opportunities, and measure their progress.

ABC data is a means to ends. It provides decision support for such activities as marginal costing. As more organizations move toward being virtual and leveraging third-party labor contractors, the management of unused capacity will become increasingly popular. Today, ABC data and its framework support the unused capacity management principles unlike any other traditional (full absorption) or nontraditional (throughput accounting) cost accounting system or methodology.

༃

> There is no question that an activity-based overhead allocation system adopts a long-run rather than a short-run focus on cost behavior. Activity costing does not imply that overhead can be saved in the short run if the transactions (activity cost drivers) that cause it are stopped. . . . The activity approach also disavows the notion that all overhead allocation is arbitrary and thus is not worth trying to do better. The approach presumes that meaningful allocation of fixed costs is possible and worth doing.
>
> *John K. Shank and Vijay Govindarajan[3]*

---

3. John K. Shank and Vijay Govindarajan, *Strategic Cost Management* (New York: The Free Press, 1993), p. 175.

CHAPTER 6

Implementation

PREPARING FOR SUCCESS

The essence of the management process is decision making—the purposeful choosing from among alternative courses of action to achieve some objective.

Charles T. Horngren[1]

Most readers of this book have read enough ABC articles or attended enough ABC seminars to know what ABC is. They must now begin building business cases for their executive decision makers in order to get approval to proceed with implementation.

6-1. THE DIFFERENCE BETWEEN IMPLEMENTATION AND INSTALLATION

ABC/ABM project managers tend to be those pioneers mentioned earlier who constantly want to dispense with the theory and fluff. They just want the how-to instruction manual. This chapter provides the instructions on how to implement an ABC/ABM system and presents some up-front decisions and caveats.

It is best to think of ABC/ABM *implementation* as preparing for the project that brings about change and ABC/ABM *installation* as setting up the software and the database interfaces. This chapter describes the implementation of ABC/ABM. Chapter 7 describes how to install an ABC/ABM system. But be forewarned before jumping ahead to read the how-to material. Attempts at ABC installation without first having success with the implementation is a recipe for failure. Implementation of ABC/ABM is more craft than science, and those readers desirous of

---

1. Charles T. Horngren, *Cost Accounting: A Managerial Emphasis* (Englewood Cliffs, NJ: Prentice Hall, 1977), p. 4.

rule-based designs, algorithms for computations, and linear regressions to optimize their ABC/ABM models had better step aside until about 1999 while an intervening generation of more practical managers apply common sense and use the insights provided by the new data to make better decisions. The craft of ABC/ABM will eventually become management science for the next generation of managers, but not right now.

6–2. IMPLEMENTATION ROADMAP

The two most often asked ABC/ABM implementation questions are, "How do I get all the way from where I am (point A, a traditional system) to get where I want to be (point B, an activity-based system)?" and "How do I get started?"

Figure 6–1 shows a highly simplified ABC/ABM implementation roadmap. The roadmap should be understood for the same reason that manufacturers plea for consumers to read their instruction guide before assembling a kit—there are things to know before getting too far along into the assembly. Otherwise, you may have regrets. The same goes here. The following describes the implementation steps presented in Figure 6–1.

Implementation Steps

- *Step 1.* Determine why you are doing ABC/ABM. What is your objective? What are the issues? What do you want changed? Who will be the end-users of the data? Meet with key end-users to validate their dissatisfaction with the current accounting practices and ensure they know how ABC/ABM will make it better. Then as you progress, have a communications plan to keep them involved.
- *Step 2.* Throw away the organization chart. Diagram the business processes at a reasonable level of detail using popular flow chart and process-mapping practices and techniques. Do not make it too summarized or too detailed. Make sure that all processes have inputs, outputs, and customers at the end. Do not overdocument the processes.
- *Step 3.* Construct and compute an ABM "strawhorse" model. Build an *activity dictionary* (preferably from the process maps; alternatively from functional department interviews) and collect

ABC/ABM Implementation Road Map

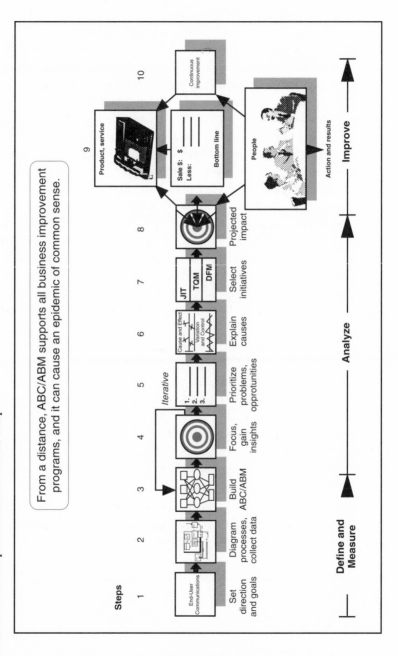

From a distance, ABC/ABM supports all business improvement programs, and it can cause an epidemic of common sense.

very high-level material and activity resource cost information based on estimates from a few good employees (or from reasonable alternative data collection techniques). Using only a single-stage cost flow, trace those resource costs into activities and group them by business processes. The ABM strawhorse model is now complete. It is that simple. Graph the data for visualization to enhance end-user interpretation, analysis, and effect.

If appropriate, further trace activity costs combined as common groups (sometimes called *activity centers*) into high-level final cost objects to better quantify ABC products, customers, and profit margins. Use only a few second-stage final activity cost drivers to keep the strawhorse simple. If useful, select an approach (e.g., impactability, value-added content, and so on—see Chapter 4) by which to score activities to bolster the analysis in step 4. This is a strawhorse process value analysis (PVA). (For a full-blown ABC model, refine and expand the model using multiple-stage cost flows with additional intermediate activity cost drivers to connect the interdependence among activities.)

- *Step 4.* Look for the problems and opportunities. Focus. Using a cross-functional team, analyze the ABM value-chain costs that have now been aligned along business processes (and also analyze profit margins if strategic ABC was done). Interpret and discuss findings. Conclude where to focus and consider what opportunities for improvement exist. Validate previously proposed improvement opportunities that are funded and already in progress. Are they valid? Don't solve problems yet.
- *Step 5.* Prioritize the opportunities for improvement.
- *Step 6.* Using popular diagnostic and analytical methods (e.g., root cause analysis), explain the causes for problems in the opportunity areas. Gain insights for alternative solutions.
- *Step 7.* Convert the opportunities into actionable management by selecting specific improvement projects and initiatives (e.g., JIT, TQM, or design for cost) that provide solutions. ABC/ABM has been called an initiative accelerator.
- *Step 8.* Using the ABC/ABM data, test the potential financial impact of each project or initiative by quantifying the cost saving,

cost avoidance, or revenue enhancement possibilities (or validate the wisdom of existing projects). Apply the planned changes to work flow and work content in the model and project the new cost behavior.

■ *Step 9.* Make changes. Proceed with altering product and service designs, changing people's attitudes, creating shared visions, restructuring work, reorganizing jobs, removing barriers, or altering the behavior of suppliers or customers. Make the processes mistake-proof .

■ *Step 10.* Are you at point B yet? If not, go back to one of the previous steps and refine. This is a continuous process, but the ABC/ABM system is a one-time construction, but always flexible in its design.

Those 10 steps are for the ABC/ABM implementation, not the installation. Steps 2 and 3 are clearly the important ones for building the ABC/ABM system. An entire ABC/ABM installation roadmap exits inside step 3. Starting in Chapter 7, expanding steps 2 and 3 will be the remaining focus of this book.

6–3. UP-FRONT DESIGN DECISIONS AND CAVEATS

It has been said that a successful ABC/ABM system implementation is 5 percent software with its interfaces and 95 percent a combination of model design and behavioral change management. This is true. Achieving success involves following classic principles recommended for managing any project:

■ Define project objectives, which will have measurable indicators as the milestones are being achieved.

■ Recognize the end-users of ABC/ABM data as internal customers and earn the right to advance with them by continuously giving them something they value, such as better data or new insights. End-users listen to radio station WIFM—*what's in it for me?* Help them to better understand through numbers a pressing business problem or a bothersome phenomenon or condition.

■ Allow the ABC/ABM system's scope, size, level of detail, granularity, and accuracy to continuously unfold by working backward from a mutually agreed-on deliverable that will help end-users solve one of their most disturbing business problems. This advice may appear counter to the TQM "do it right the first time" philosophy, but rapid prototyping as a learning device for adults is just a better, more expedient, and more practical approach. ABC/ABM system implementations usually stumble when they are overengineered and are without a predefined purpose.

Refer to Figure 6–2. Start with a noncomputerized, grease pencil drawing of your organization's ABC/ABM multistage cost flow model before constructing your spreadsheet strawhorse. The myriad of up-front ABC/ABM installation-related questions about the number of cost drivers, the number of activities, the choice of cost drivers, the frequency of model updates, and so on are ultimately best answered by first gaining experience and then constantly satisfying the internal customer's needs and wants.

The next three sections describe each point above. Then Chapter 7 expands only on steps 2 and 3 from the implementation roadmap. These two steps comprise the installation roadmap.

A decision must be made as to whether the first ABC/ABM model is intended as a diagnostic one-time study, a baseline for a repeatable model, or a fully integrated and automated permanent production system. These three choices are depicted along a continuum in Figure 6–3.

Regardless of where on the continuum you choose to begin, you still have to satisfy the issues previously mentioned. How to do so will be discussed in the next three sections.

6–4. DEFINING OBJECTIVES FOR SUCCESS— YARDSTICK MEASURES

ABC/ABM projects can fall short of their full potential. To succeed you must do more than just (1) understand why ABC/ABM projects don't totally satisfy objectives, (2) learn from those lessons, and (3) take corrective actions to not repeat others' implementation errors. Although those are noble goals, it is worth proactively establishing in advance your own yardstick measures for success of your own ABC/ABM project.

Common barriers to successful ABC/ABM implementation relate to accountability in two very different ways. One way previously discussed involves the initial resistance of internal end-users caused by anxieties that their performance may be financially measured with techniques other than the traditional measures they've artfully mastered over the

FIGURE 6 – 2

Conditions for Successful Implementation

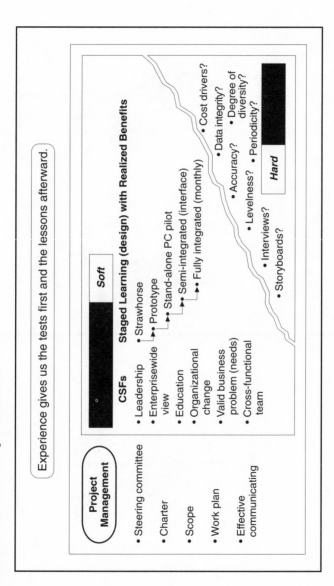

FIGURE 6 – 3

ABC/ABM Implementation Continuum

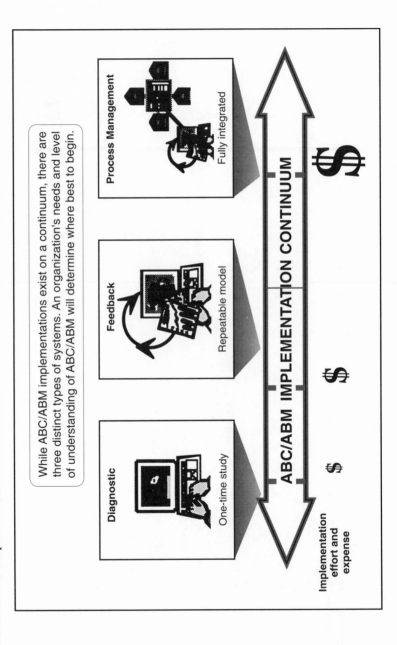

While ABC/ABM implementations exist on a continuum, there are three distinct types of systems. An organization's needs and level of understanding of ABC/ABM will determine where best to begin.

Diagnostic — One-time study

Feedback — Repeatable model

Process Management — Fully integrated

ABC/ABM IMPLEMENTATION CONTINUUM

Implementation effort and expense

years. But the second problem involves monitoring the ABC/ABM implementation project itself. How is the ABC/ABM project's success to be measured? Too often it isn't. Who is to be held accountable? How?

During the fall of 1993, the CAM-I ABC/ABM Practitioners' Group brainstormed these issues, asking themselves, "If my ABC/ABM project is being successful, how would I know it?" Their task was to develop measurable indicators of success. The results are summarized in Figure 6–4.

FIGURE 6 – 4

Measuring Success

How to measure success.

Question

If the ABC/ABM pilot is being successful, how would we know it?

Answers

- The business starts being managed differently.
- The pilot progresses to a next phase.
- End-user interest and requests for feedback increase.
- The new data starts being used and acted on.
- An ABC lanaguage emerges among employees.

Question

What would be measurable indicators of a pilot's success?

Answers

- Cycle times are reduced and quality is increased.
- Performance measurements are reformed with a greater emphasis along business processes.
- Other continuous improvement programs request or use the ABC/ABM data.
- Additional improvement projects are stimulated.
- A second ABC/ABM pilot is endorsed.
- The number of ABC literate end-users expands.
- The number of decision applications using ABC data expands.
- A survey of nonfinancial end-users indicates satisfaction with the system.
- Additional executive-level sponsors appear.
- Requests for ABC/ABM training increase.
- ABC model updates are frequently requested.
- Products become more profitable.

Interestingly, the success measures did not directly include the amount of reduced or avoided costs. The dominant success indicators looked to the behavior of end-users, including their frequency of use of the data and their accelerating rate of learning.

6–5. EARNING THE RIGHT TO ADVANCE WITH END-USERS

Success begets future successes. An ABC/ABM implementation is not a sprint like a 100-meter foot race. It is more like a chess game, or like coaxing a cat (the internal customer) out of a hiding spot. One has to think ahead, determine ways to constantly produce value, hold the internal end-users' ongoing interest, and eventually wind up with a fully erected, permanent and repeatable ABC/ABM production system. The important advice is to *achieve successes along the way,* that is, earn the right to advance.

However, remember that there is a clock ticking once the ABC/ABM project has started. End-users can sense if a project is losing momentum. Regardless of an ABC/ABM project's merits, users will lose interest if they are not getting anything in return that they deem of value. Here is the solution to maintain momentum: As the new data become available, schedule "discovery" presentations to stir the end-users' curiosity, sustain their interest, and obtain further direction from their feedback. You do not necessarily have to present conclusions and recommendations. Just show them your findings.

6–6. POPULAR APPLICATIONS OF ABC/ABM DATA

Since ABC/ABM data are basically used as means to an end, it is important identify the "end." Agree on a decision capability for the new data that the end-users have really wanted and that will give them positive results when they finally use it.

Do not underestimate resistance to change. There is a phrase, "Better the devil you know than the devil you don't know." People will resist reforms to measures even if they know that the one's they're using are bad because they also know how to get around them for personal purposes. Foster support for good data for everybody in order to stop perpetuating bad decisions based on flawed data. Circumvent any barriers to change. ABC/ABM proponents strongly believe that the use of activity-based costing data and its associated practices is an eventuality.

What kinds of decisions do end-users base on financial information? What are the most popular applications for ABC/ABM data? Here's an unscientifically rank-ordered list assembled from the decision capabilities from Figure 3–5, which appeared in Chapter 3.

Strategic Applications	Operational Applications
How to conduct business?	Where to look for opportunities?
■ Order quotations (pricing)	■ Business process/activity value analysis
■ Product profitability analysis	■ Cost-of-quality analysis
■ Customer profitability analysis	■ Cost driver analysis (unit cost of outputs)
■ Capital expenditure justifications	■ Make-or-buy analysis
■ Performance measurements	■ Business process reengineering
■ Target costing	■ Benchmarking
■ Life-cycle costing	■ Activity-based budgeting
	■ Unused capacity analysis

Regardless of which end-users you choose to delight and which decision-making application you bolster for them, always try to keep the initial design of the ABC/ABM model relatively simple and prevent from overengineering it. Always look for ways to summarize the detail in a way that enhances decision-making power. Refine and expand the model later.

6–7. CRITICAL SUCCESS FACTORS FOR ABC/ABM IMPLEMENTATIONS

The key to successful implementation and sustained use of the ABC data is to balance the four areas presented in Figure 6–5:

1. ABC model design and architecture—Constructing an ABC/ABM model combines art, craft, and science.
2. Implementation and integration—It is important to select promising pilot sites and to involve individuals with information-technology skills.
3. Getting buy-in—Get the support of an executive sponsor and create widespread interest in and ownership of the data and its uses.
4. Application of the data—Be sure there are end-users with strong needs for the ABC/ABM data.

FIGURE 6 – 5

Factors for the Successful Implementation of ABC/ABM

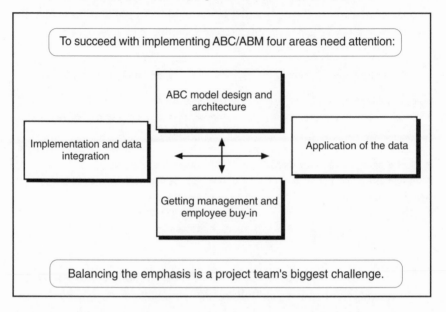

Figure 6–6 expands on elements to consider in balancing the four areas of emphasis.

The next chapter focuses on steps 2 and 3 of the ABC/ABM implementation roadmap.

Poor management accounting systems, by themselves, will not lead to organizational failure. Nor will excellent management accounting systems assure success. But they certainly can contribute to the decline or survival of organizations.

H. Thomas Johnson and Robert S. Kaplan[2]

Cost objectives are chosen not for their own sake but to facilitate decisions. The most economically feasible approach to the design of a cost system is to assume some common class of decisions, such as inventory control, and to choose cost objectives . . . that relate to those decisions.

Charles T. Horngren[3]

2. H. Thomas Johnson and Robert S. Kaplan, *Relevance Lost: The Rise and Fall of Management Accounting* (Boston, MA: Harvard Business School Press, 1987), p. 261.
3. Charles T. Horngren, *Cost Accounting: A Managerial Emphasis* (Englewood Cliffs, NJ: Prentice Hall, 1977), p. 20.

Elements of ABC/ABM Success Factors

Application of Data

- Profitability analysis
- Focus for improvements
- Process value analysis
- Target costing
- Unused capacity management
- Benchmarking
- Predictive planning
- Price quotations
- Investment justification
- Budgeting
- Process changes
- Strategy changes

Model Design and Architecture

- Level of complexity
- Level of detail
- Cost drivers
- Accuracy requirements
- Activity definitions
- Process linkages

Getting Buy-In

- Executive sponsorship
- Project champion
- Overcoming resistance
- Credibility of outputs
- Not accounting-driven
- Creating ownership

Implementation/Integration

- Scope and boundaries
- Pilot site choice and phasing
- ABC/ABM software
- Data interfaces
- Data collection approaches
- Single versus dual systems
- Validation of the data

CHAPTER 7

Implementation

AN ABC/ABM INSTALLATION
ROADMAP

To some it may be unnecessary to discuss the difference between a program of distributing overhead to costs by means of normal (at standard) overhead rates and one of absorbing all current overhead into cost regardless of the volume of production, yet I am sure that many manufacturers still use the latter unscientific and dangerous method.

C. B. Williams[1]

7–1. ABM AS AN
ATTENTION-DIRECTING MECHANISM

Figure 6–2 advocated using a staged-learning approach for adults to accelerate buy-in, reduce resistance to change, and gain increasingly wider acceptance of the ABC/ABM concepts. Staged learning allows for flexibly modifying the ABC/ABM model to meet end-users' needs prior to the model becoming too large and complicated. A popular ABC/ABM installation approach (and which heavily expands on steps 2 and 3 of the instruction manual) includes:

- Identify core business processes by creating enterprisewide diagrams (relationship maps) (7–3).
- Build business process maps as supplier value chains (7–4).
- Identify the activities central and tangent to the core business processes (7–5).
- Organize to collect the resource cost consumption data for activities (7–6).

1. C. B. Williams, "The Distribution of Overhead under Abnormal Conditions," *National Association of Cost Accountants (NACA) Yearbook,* 1921.

- Add new activities as needed to capture 100 percent of the resource time being consumed (7–7).
- Measure or estimate labor costs (7–8).
- Measure or estimate purchased material and service costs (7–9).
- Trace activity costs to intermediate and to final cost objects (7–10).
- Reconfigure the cost data and visualize the business processes (7–11).
- Analyze costs for insights and take actions (7–12).

Traditional cost accounting reports expenditures to managers by department or cost center. As earlier mentioned, this simply gives managers and employees a silo or stovepipe view of themselves and actually blocks them from seeing how their enterprise behaves horizontally by processes and as a total business system. In effect, traditional, general ledger cost accounting systems act like thick cloud covers. The clouds prevent any observation, and eventual understanding, of the locations and rates at which the enterprise uses resources to enable the creation of value or to actually create value for customers (see Figure 7–1).

What managers initially need is a quick glimpse of what's below those clouds. Traditional accounting systems provide little visibility to business processes, and managers need to understand costs of these processes. These dismal conditions justify why ABM supply value-chain cost data need only be collected and initially reported using a fast, high-altitude "flyover" technique—dip under those clouds and snap a few pictures of the enterprise's cost use and then interpret what is seen. This high-altitude flyover in effect becomes the strawhorse mock-up for the eventual ABC/ABM cost system.

The flyover approach to collect data can be accomplished quickly, painlessly, and with little invasive impact on employees. And this can be done in days, not months. The reason to do this is to discover and learn. The purpose for the ABM data is strictly as an attention-directing diagnostic. This ABM costs snapshot is not meant to win buy-in from employees yet. It is also not intended to solve problems or assign costs to outputs yet. All of that comes later. It simply creates an illustration of what an enterprise's business processes look like in shape and size and is strictly designed to stimulate and answer some basic questions:

- Just where in the core business processes are costs significantly adding up to enable and to create value? At what rate of cost accumulation?

FIGURE 7-1

Learn and Discover in Phases and by Doing

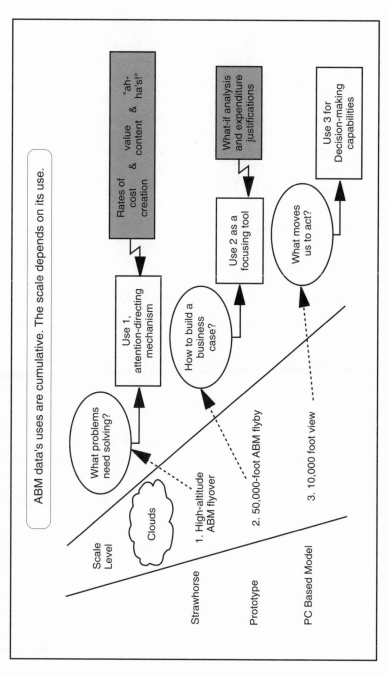

- How well do the relative cost magnitudes of the core business processes align with senior management's strategies and objectives? Is there surprisingly little spending on items management has claimed are strategically critical?
- How do the new facts match or validate everyone's beliefs of the current operating state of the business?
- What is the value creating content of activities (e.g., rated from lowest to highest) along each core business process? Which activities are more important? Which activities do we perform well or poorly? Which activities are more easily impactable? Less easily impactable? Who is receiving the value? Where is there waste?

Senior managers are asking these quesitons. Will they like the answers ABM provides? When the truth is known, will a significant amount of costs not be supporting the primary missions of the enterprise? Are their organizations temporarily disadvantaged or truly bad? With the high-altitude flyover ABM model, facts finally begin to replace opinions and assertions.

7–2. ABM AS A FOCUSING TOOL

Supplier value-chain analysis (ABM) at a high-altitude flyover stimulates managers and employees. Finding the answers to the above questions ignites them to build strong business cases to take actions. In this way, ABM achieves its purpose as an attention-directing mechanism.

Building compelling business cases, however, may require more specifics and particulars than provided by the high-altitude flyover snapshots. A better, closer view gained from a 50,000-foot ABM flyby can help managers focus on the specific core business processes. At a granular level, with more code-indented activity levels, the processes' cost consumption characteristics will provide greater resolution, become more visible, and be even better understood by end-users. Revisit Figure 6–1; at this point you can go from step 4 back to step 3 to refine the ABM model.

By collecting lower-level, decomposed activity cost data, more hidden costs, likely to be favorably affected by a future process change, can be identified and quantified. The sum of the hidden costs of the core business processes, when scored and combined with the more obvious non-value and low-value-adding activity costs, may well tip the scales in a decision of whether or not to proceed with an improvement initiative or investment.

The ABM value-chain activity analysis can be further magnified with a more detailed and illuminating 10,000-foot flyby. This data collection and reporting exercise can also be quick and economical, accomplished in days, not months.

Although this approach based on estimates may not seem initially credible regardless of the low "altitude," end-users' doubts may be alleviated when they think through how the further decomposition of cost information increases its accuracy. Virtually all the properties of the activity cost data hold constant as you decompose or telescope the model's activities downward. The totality of the enterprisewide activity costs always remains at a constant dollar amount, and so do the core business processes. The total costs don't change; only their detail does. Also, the very nature and definition of the activities may change to include not necessarily more but a different flavor of activities.

Okay! Let's begin traveling down the ABC/ABM installation roadmap which includes steps 2 and 3 from Figure 6–1.

7–3. ABC/ABM BEGINS WITH ENTERPRISEWIDE DIAGRAMS

The starting point of the installation roadmap is to identify business processes. A popular approach for identifying them is to use visual diagrams. This is a top-down approach.

At an overarching level, as depicted in Figure 7–2, an organization operates as a total system. It exploits its core competencies by anticipating customers' needs and wants and designing products and processes to deliver and sustain customer satisfaction.

Ten years ago you could not show your boss a diagram like Figure 7–3. It looks complicated; it has that foreign, electronic data processing appearance to it. Your boss' immediate reaction 10 years ago would have been that the diagram was either conceptual or theoretical and not in the "hands on and make things (anything) happen" mode that many ready-fire-aim bosses like. Today, we have a new generation of managers who have grown-up and been trained with a systemic view of approaching matters. They acknowledge and appreciate how a business is comprised

FIGURE 7-2

Processes Deliver Value to Customers

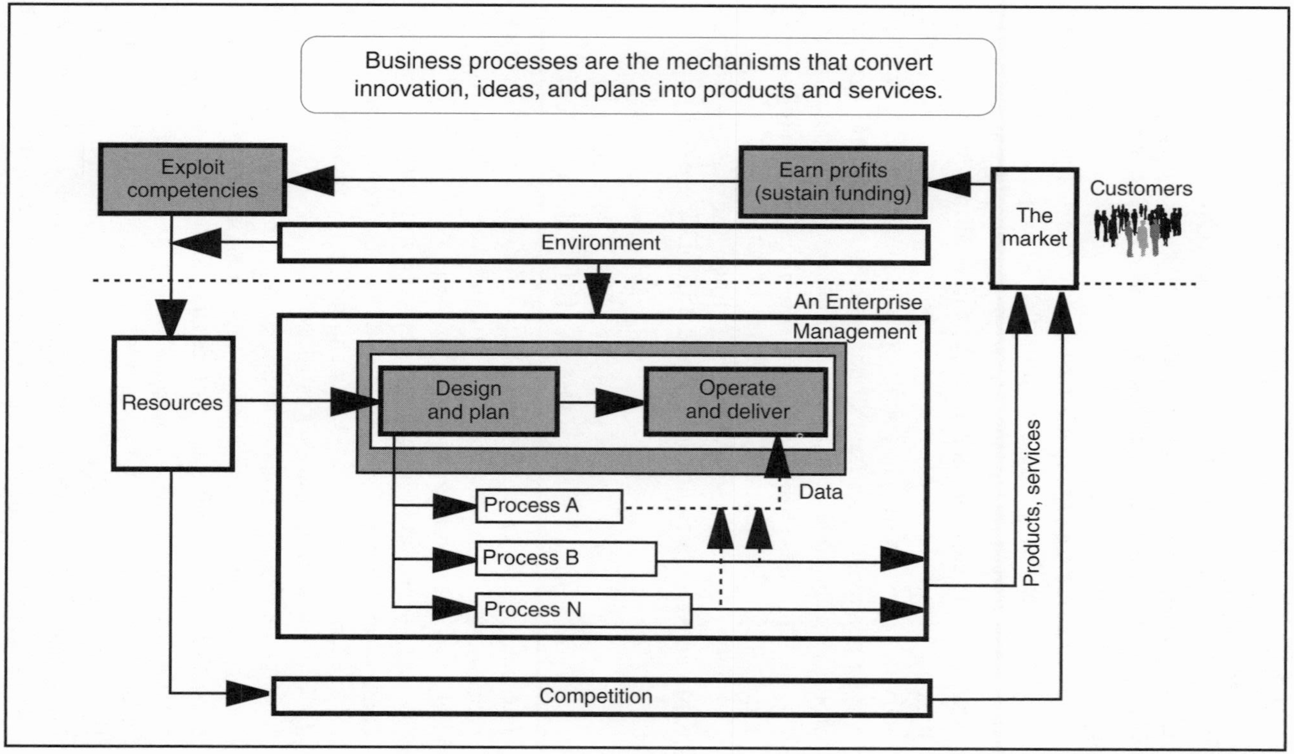

Business processes are the mechanisms that convert innovation, ideas, and plans into products and services.

Enterprise Relationship Map

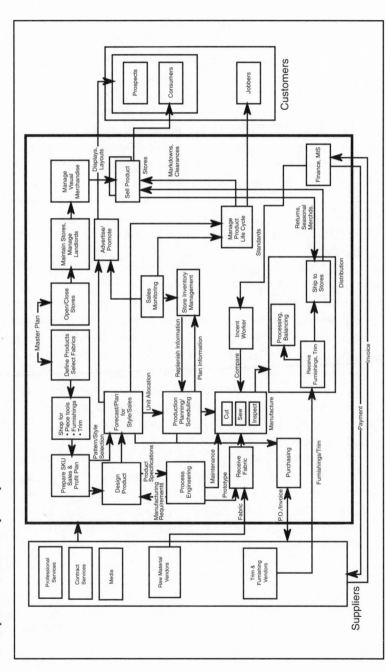

of interconnected activities. These managers can handle such diagrams, which are called *organizational relationship maps.* Holistic thinking is now acceptable managerial behavior—managers are beginning to understand that their business operates as a total system.

Relationship maps are not really new—computer programmers and information systems managers have relied on variations of these graphics, called *entity-relationship diagrams* (ERDs) and *data flow diagrams* (DFDs), to write computer codes. In the world of automated information systems, these tools have helped technical software programmers to better understand businesspeople's needs and wants. Tools and techniques like relationship maps and diagrams fall under a broader description called *structured systems* and *application program development.* Organizational relationship maps have now become acceptable in business because they help in identifying business processes and managing behavioral change.

Without getting too complicated, the relationship maps in Figures 7–4 and 7–5 show what people do as they interact as a total organization and how they relate to others outside their functional, stovepipe boundaries. The entire enterprise or total organization lies within the dark, bold border. External suppliers and customers are outside of the border. By viewing the relationship maps as supply chains from left to right, we see that first the resources (such as people, equipment, materials, utilities, and financial capital) are inputed into the bold-bordered enterprise. Within the enterprise, those resources are converted into products and services and provided to external customers, or "receivers."

Simply stated, any organization inside the dark border has two activities: (1) receive request from a customer and (2) fulfill that request. Beyond those are the support activities of creating customer demand and administering the organization's activities. The relationship map can be decomposed to reveal deeper relationships between organizational activities. A relationship map is in effect a comprehensive model of how an enterprise enables the creation of, creates, and adds value across the supply chains in industry and commerce. Refer to Figure 7–6. Relationship maps help employees and managers to think about their business as a total system. In fact, it is a system comprised of only a few core business processes. The map helps identify the work done (i.e., the product), who the work is for (i.e., the customer), and what is

Relationship Mapping

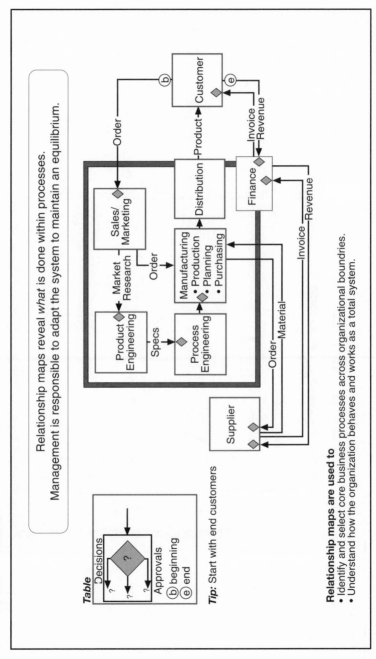

Relationship maps reveal *what* is done within processes.
Management is responsible to adapt the system to maintain an equilibrium.

Table

Decisions

Approvals
ⓑ beginning
ⓔ end

Tip: Start with end customers

Relationship maps are used to
• Identify and select core business processes across organizational boundries.
• Understand how the organization behaves and works as a total system.

155

F I G U R E 7 – 5

Decomposed Relationship Map: A Manufacturer

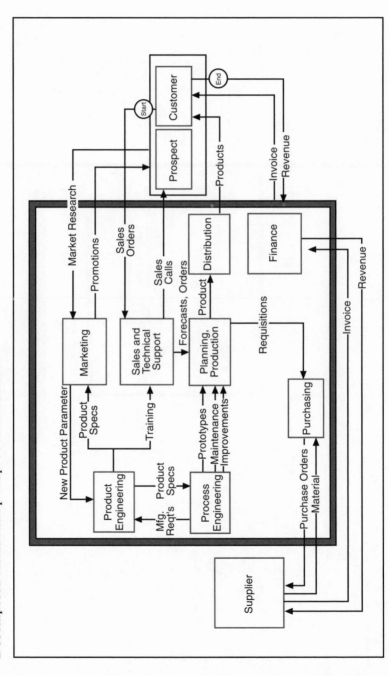

Relationship Mapping to Understand Creating Value

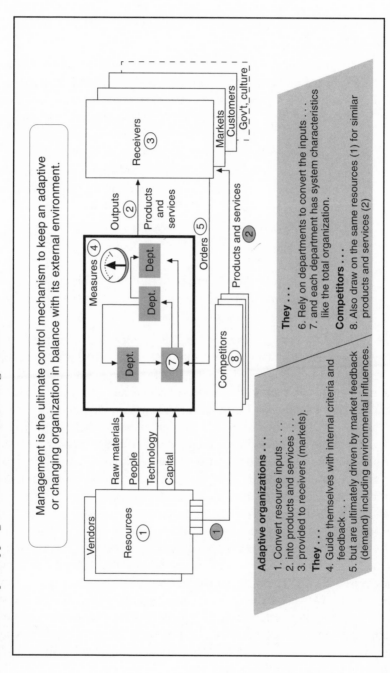

Management is the ultimate control mechanism to keep an adaptive or changing organization in balance with its external environment.

Adaptive organizations . . .
1. Convert resource inputs . . . . .
2. into products and services . . .
3. provided to receivers (markets).

They . . .
4. Guide themselves with internal criteria and feedback . . . .
5. but are ultimately driven by market feedback (demand) including environmental influences.

They . . . .
6. Rely on departments to convert the inputs . . . .
7. and each department has system characteristics like the total organization.

Competitors . . .
8. Also draw on the same resources (1) for similar products and services (2)

Source: Geary Rummler and Alan Branche, *Improving Performance: How to Manage the White Space on the Organization Chart*, Figure 2.4, p. 10. Copyright 1995 by Jossey-Bass Inc., Publishers.

needed to accomplish the work (i.e., the supplier). There are additional insights gained from using this kind of thinking along with the relationship map:

- Inside the bold border, a few prominent business processes (e.g., from customer order placement to cash payment following product delivery) circulate like large protruding veins and carry accumulated value along the way. *These are the internal supplier value-chains.*

- It is senior management's responsibility to keep the bold-bordered enterprise in balance and equilibrium in response to all of the influences from its external environment (e.g., customers, competitors, new technologies, or governments).

- Competitors can also draw on the same resources to satisfy the same receivers. (To many companies, this is a scary but true observation.)

- In order for the bold-bordered enterprise to continuously enable and create value, it must be adaptive and constantly change. And customer sales must ultimately exceed costs.

The relationship map is not a system design tool; it is a management of change tool. Here is why. As vice presidents, department managers, and other "silo and stovepipe" supervisors selfishly squint at their own company's relationship map to try to locate subordinate employees under their fiefdom, they usually can't find them inside any single box. Only fractions of "their" people are in boxes; and they are in lots of boxes, but each employee is totally accounted for. Today's employees are literally all over the map, negotiating with a customer one hour, contributing to a new product or service development idea another hour, and troubleshooting a nonconformance or process-defect problem another hour. And as companies further de-layer and flatten their organization structure, this fragmentation and dispersion of individuals across business processes is intensifying.

The "management of change" contribution from the relationship map comes from the way the map reinforces the pressure on managers to think enterprisewide and cross-functionally, to tip over their stovepipe attitudes and views, and to help collectively manage their enterprise as a total system.

One note of caution should be made. As the relationship map eventually gets further decomposed, that is, more detailed and intricate, it begins turning off the very target audience you want tuning in to it. Therefore, keep the relationship map at a summary level without getting too detailed. Aim for the sweet spot, like on a tennis racket, somewhere between too complex and too simple. It is a top-down tool. In section 7–5 we'll integrate ABC/ABM data to the map as a bottom-up tool.

7–4. LINKING ABM TO RELATIONSHIP MAPS USING PROCESS MAPPING

Process mapping is synonymous with value-chain analysis. It helps to document the results of the relationship map and organize information to ensure it is complete, understandable, and readily analyzable. ABM reconfigures the organization and assigns costs to business processes, something that traditional accounting cannot achieve.

Until the next generation of managers, relationship diagrams and business process maps should probably be kept at a summary level. They will need to be graphically modeled and visualized at an intermediate-to-high level. Fortunately, this is the same level at which ABM costs should be collected, measured, and reported. (There is little to be gained by costing the tasks that make up activities; it is too detailed.) Therefore, the cost data can be aligned with processes and maintained in sync with the messages that are signaled to managers from the relationship map.

Remember that a business process is comprised of two or more activities. A business process is defined as a sequence or network of logically related work activities structured to provide outputs for customers. These business processes provide the building blocks through which the organization creates value for its customers. Figure 7–7 describes business processes.

FIGURE 7 – 7

Business Processes

A process is a sequence or network of logically related work activities structured to provide a specific output, usually customer-directed.

- Functional names often disguise the core processes that are cross-functional.
- Groups of activites are often not recognized as a core process.
- A company's core processes are small in number.
- Processes exist across organizations.
- A process output may be measured in terms of quality, flexibility, delivery schedule, cycle time, and cost.
- Somebody must own each process; but someone rarely does.

7–5. IDENTIFYING ACTIVITIES WITHIN BUSINESS PROCESSES

How does one identify and define which activities to quantify? Regardless of an organization's size or number of employees, a virtually limitless number of activities can be selected. How do you control the size and number of activities? The criteria for identification of activities should include materiality as well as the objectives of the ABC/ABM data discussed in step 1 of the implementation roadmap.

You can maintain materiality by using common sense. Don't chase details. Strategic objectives for ABC/ABM can require identifying and defining more summarized levels of activities than if the objectives are tactical and simply for operational improvement. For example, strategic uses of ABC/ABM data such as for product and customer profitability analysis or for sales order quotations require accurately tracing cost diversity to final cost objects. For those strategic purposes, activities can be broadly defined in terms of commonalties. If, on the other hand, the intent is cost reduction or future cost avoidance, activities should be defined more granularly, with attention on waste elimination and low-value-added work, like reworking or double-checking an order.

How detailed should one get in defining activities? A good rule is to think of activities as what people do and the tasks that make up activities as how the people perform activities. Task definitions can be included for purposes of improvement, but costs of task performance should not be measured and put into the activity-based accounting system. It is also important to put some pain into the activity dictionary. Be sure to define those activities that people would like to see disappear even though they are necessary. This builds emotion and electrically charges the ABC/ABM model.

7–6. ORGANIZING TO COLLECT RESOURCE COST DATA BY ACTIVITIES

The ABC/ABM system must initially assign resource costs to activities. Resource costs are continuously captured via transactions in general ledger journal account balances (e.g., payroll, accounts payable, material stores issues, journal entries, and so forth). The assignment of these costs to activities can be done:

- By direct charging, using existing measurements (e.g., charging repairs via a work order, metering fuel consumption, charging supply issues).

- By estimation (i.e., by questionnaire or surveying techniques).
- With arbitrary allocations; but these should clearly be resisted because they do not aid in better understanding or modeling the economics of the business.

Direct charging with measured data consumed by its cost object is common sense. However, dealing with indirect charges requires identifying activities and estimating the labor and material consumption within each. Figure 7–8 shows three options for estimating indirect costs. It is easiest to collect data on labor and service-time costs before estimating external purchased material and contractor service costs. The reason is that concentrating first on what people do (for other people) defines a basis on which purchased materials and contractor services can subsequently be assigned. How to estimate costs of purchased materials and services is addressed in Section 7–9.

Estimating can be controversial because it implies there will be some degree of error. With ABC, however, knowledgeable estimates from informed individuals are much more preferable than precise calculations of irrelevant allocations.

The first of the three estimating options relies on business process supply chains as the source for defining activities. Using a predefined process map, which arranges the organization into a network of labor-performing work, simplifies defining activities. At the lowest step of each business process, simply describe a few (two to five) verb-adjective-noun activities. Repeat this for every step of every business process, and you'll eventually construct the activity dictionary. Refer to Figure 7–9A. (Also see misconception 3 in Chapter 8.)

The second estimating option is useful when there are incomplete or no documented business process flow charts. This option creates the whole (i.e., the processes) from the sum of the parts (i.e., the work activities). Each stovepipe, functional department is surveyed for the employees' activities in isolation of the other departments. When all departments have been surveyed, the activity-based model (whether ABM or ABC) for the total enterprise is then created by assembling the parts into a whole. Each functional estimator is like a lamppost in a previously dark parking lot. Together, the light from all of the lampposts produces visibility of the entire parking lot, without any dark spots. The business processes are rationalized from examining the verb-adjective-noun activities, and then these activities are sequenced along the business

FIGURE 7–8

Tracing Indirect Support Costs

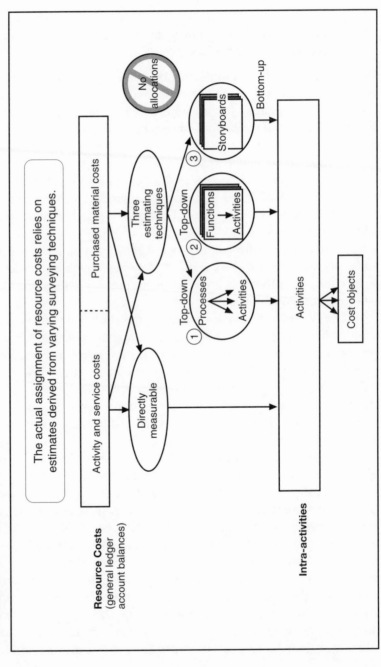

processes. (More complex business processes tend to be weblike networks, not sequential nodes; but regardless of how activities relate to each other, the estimating technique to identify and define activities is unaffected.)

Figure 7–9B shows a time-effort input form that has been completed by a functional representative. The estimates have been rounded to 5 percent increments.

Figure 7–9C shows the costed activities, with average salary and fringe rates used for each natural work group; the total costs appear in the last column.

Both of the above options are designed to produce rapid, noninvasive results with a minimum adverse impact on data accuracy and credibility. Both techniques are top-down and rely on a few good employees as representative estimators (see Figure 7–10). That is, the ratio of employees to estimators is high. ABC/ABM implementation teams frequently rotate back and forth between these two options as empty holes of work-content get defined and filled in. These two estimating options check and balance one another because they both are describing the same thing: the work people do.

The top-down approach to achieve quick availability and visibility of activity-based cost data is more effective when the number of functional representative estimators (i.e., the few good employees) is limited, they reasonably understand their business, and a financial accounting (or budgeting) team member is knowledgeable about general ledger accounts and balances.

The third estimating option is a bottom-up, small group technique that relies on storyboarding. Storyboarding employs cut-and-paste bits of information and flip charts and involves intense participation of work groups. It relies on numerous group meetings of side-by-side employees in which they define what they do and how they do it. This technique supports total quality management (TQM) improvement philosophies. Each team member of every work team formally defines work from his or her viewpoint. The employees' time is then apportioned to their known activities, and the costs are assembled in a manner similar to that used in the second option.

In practice, companies with successful ABC/ABM systems have used elements from all three of these data collection options. The advantage of the first two options is the data can be rapidly collected with relatively high accuracy, consistent definitions, and

FIGURE 7-9A

Activities Translate Ledger into Process Costs

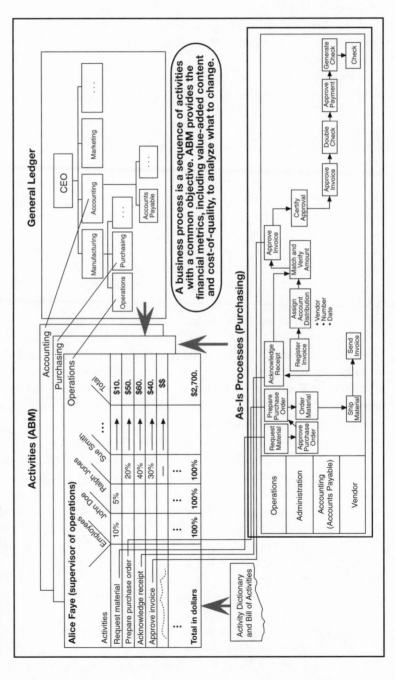

FIGURE 7-9 B

Time-Effort Input Sheet

Employee and Expense Activity Effort Worksheet (%)

		Prepared by Project Manager:		Date:		Page ___ of ___	
		Employee Names/#/Groups & Expenses					
Activity / Avg. Wage & No. Employees	3 @ $20K Material Handlers	2 @ $20K Inspectors	2 @ $35K Maintenance	2 @ $25K Computer Programmers	1 @ $45K Scheduler	2 @ 50K Set-up Engineers	3 @ $50K Printers
Set-up equipment						90%	10%
Chase material	25%						
Inspect finished cards		50%					
Inspect incoming material		50%					
Maintain facility			30%				
Manage program changes				75%			
Move material	50%				25%	10%	
Plan printing schedule				25%	75%		
Store excess material	25%						
Do unscheduled maintenance			40%				
Run 1972 standard printer			25%				60%
Run 1995 personalized printer			5%				30%
Total	100%	100%	100%	100%	100%	100%	100%

FIGURE 7-9C

Costed Activities

Employee and Expense Activity Effort Worksheet ($)

Prepared by Project Manager: ___ Date: ___ Page ___ of ___

Activity / No. Employees	3 Material Handlers	2 Inspectors	2 Maintenance	2 Computer Programmers	1 Scheduler	2 Set-up Engineers	3 Printers	Total
Set-up equipment						$90,000		$90,000
Chase material	$15,000						$15,000	$30,000
Inspect finished cards		$20,000						$20,000
Inspect incoming material		$20,000						$20,000
Maintain facility			$21,000					$21,000
Manage program changes				$37,500				$37,500
Move material	$30,000				$11,250	$10,000		$51,250
Plan printing schedule				$12,500	$33,750			$46,250
Store excess material	$15,000							$15,000
Do unscheduled maintenance			$28,000					$28,000
Run 1972 standard printer			$17,500				$90,000*	$107,500
Run 1995 personalized printer			$3,500				$45,000*	$48,500
Total	$60,000	$40,000	$70,000	$50,000	$45,000	$100,000	$150,000	$515,000

Employee Names/#/Groups & Expenses

*$135,000 direct labor cost

Rapid Labor Effect Data Collection

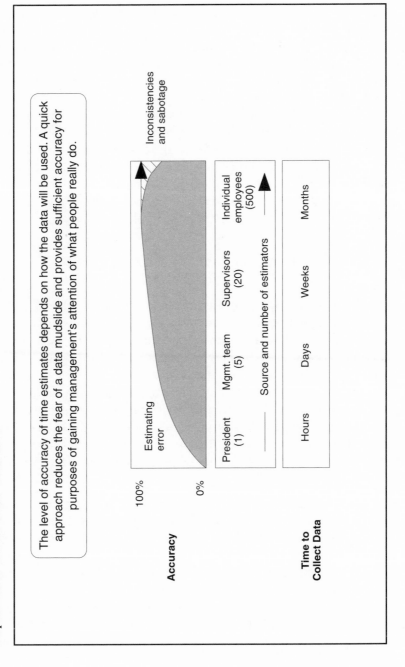

initial noninvasive impact on employees. The advantage of the story-boarding option is there is greater employee involvement, which helps change personal attitudes, may speed achievement of consensus and minimizes resistance to change. Regardless of which technique you use, be sensitive to the individuals who are being honest about the organizations activities. Do not make it a job-threatening experience. ABC data must be used responsibly.

Labor conversion costs can be estimated using an apportioning method or a cycle-time method. The first approach accounts for 100 percent of the total time required for all the organization's activities, breaking down each worker's time as a percentage of that total. The cycle-time method relies on time-based output measures, like the number of minutes to process an order. The next section describes the percent approach. Section 7–8, which follows it, describes the cycle-time approach.

7–7. MEASURING LABOR CONVERSION COSTS BY PERCENT

As earlier described, the high-altitude flyover and low-altitude flyby data collection approaches provide increased, scalable information (i.e., more granular) and without distortion. This data can then be used to measure labor conversion costs. Employees' average salary and fringe benefit dollars are multiplied by the estimated percentage of the total work that the employees' activities account for. Average salaries can be identified at the same department levels as used during the annual budget exercise.

In practice, gaining estimating accuracy through scaling is accomplished by merely expanding the size of the activity-by-employee-group matrix or using more work representative estimators. Here are ways to get more accuracy:

- The number of natural work groups that are estimated for can be further subdivided, but the total number of employees will always remain the same. Natural work groups are two or more employees, not necessarily from the same department, who perform common activities with related outputs, like purchasing agents and receiving dock workers. Note that despite subdividing, the ratio of total employees to estimators remains unchanged.

- The verb-adjective-noun activity convention remains unaffected, but the lowest-level activity column can be expanded by adding an indented column to the activity dictionary, thus providing another level in detail. Here the ratio of employees to estimators is still unchanged.
- The number of functional representative estimators can be doubled or tripled to achieve a more accurate estimate of the incrementally lower level of costs from the further subdivided natural work groups of employees. This lowers the ratio of employees to estimators. More estimators assure a greater familiarity with how work time is apportioned by the employees within natural work groups.

Remember, as you expand scale and decompose the activities, the total of dollars accounted for in the cost snapshot does not change. Total costs are not newly created or destroyed. Only the clarity of the picture changes with a higher resolution of detail or expanded segmentation caused by diversity. Figure 7–11 presents an example using landscape workers of how estimating accuracy increases through scaling.

7–8. MEASURING LABOR CONVERSION COSTS BY CYCLE-TIME OUTPUTS

The cycle-time approach requires a start-to-end process flow chart. An average cycle time is estimated for each activity, or group of activities. For example, assume that travel reservationists handle completed ticket reservations and customer inquiries about schedule times, departures, arrivals, or ticket prices. Also assume the following:

Average time per completed reservation	= 7.50 minutes/output
Number of completed reservations per month	= 10,000
Average time per inquiry	= 4.00 minutes/output
Number of inquiries per month	= 19,650
Number of travel reservationists	= 20
Average monthly salary and fringe/employee	= $3,000
Average employee hours worked/week	= 40.0 hours
Average break time per worker/week	= 8.0 hours

FIGURE 7-11

Accuracy Trade-Offs

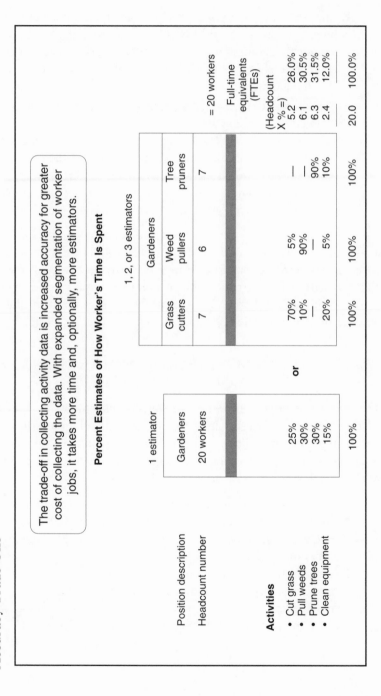

The trade-off in collecting activity data is increased accuracy for greater cost of collecting the data. With expanded segmentation of worker jobs, it takes more time and, optionally, more estimators.

Percent Estimates of How Worker's Time Is Spent

1 estimator

Position description	Gardeners
Headcount number	20 workers
Activities	
• Cut grass	25%
• Pull weeds	30%
• Prune trees	30%
• Clean equipment	15%
	100%

or

1, 2, or 3 estimators

Position description	Grass cutters	Weed pullers	Tree pruners	= 20 workers	
		Gardeners		Full-time equivalents (FTEs)	
Headcount number	7	6	7	(Headcount X % =)	
Activities					
• Cut grass	70%	5%	—	5.2	26.0%
• Pull weeds	10%	90%	—	6.1	30.5%
• Prune trees	—	—	90%	6.3	31.5%
• Clean equipment	20%	5%	10%	2.4	12.0%
	100%	100%	100%	20.0	100.0%

A cost per completed reservation and per inquiry can be computed as follows:

$3,000 salary and fringe   40 hours/week
     × 20 employees   –   8 hours/week break time
$60,000 payroll per month   32 hours
                                     ×   4 weeks/month
                                       128 hours/month
                                     × 20 employees
                                     2,560 person-hours/month

Cost factor = $60,000 (load)/2,560 (rate)
            = $23.4375/hour
            = $.390625/minute

Cost per completed reservation @ 7.5 minutes = $2.9296875
Cost per inquiry @ 4.0 minutes = $1.5625

One of the complications with the cycle-time output approach is reconciling the total costs. By continuing with the cost math:

10,000 reservations @ $2.929687 each = $29,296.87
19,650 inquires @ $1.5625 each   = $30,703.13
                                         $60,000.00

But I have rigged this example for the numbers to come out exactly. That is, all of the input date (i.e., payroll dollars, break time, employee attendance, quantity of transactions) were assumed to be known in advance prior to the month's actual results. This allows for the cost-load rates and average cycle-times to precisely reconcile the total $60,000 cost.

A more realistic example would have possibly measured a different mix of transactions, say 9,100 reservations and 20,100 inquiries. Since the cost-load rate ($23.4375/hours) and average transaction cycle-times are usually always standard measures based on prior historical data, the actual incurred dollars will never reconcile the ABC/ABM model's costs:

9,100 reservations @ $2.929687 each   = $26,660.15
20,100 inquiries @ $1.5625 each   =   31,406.25
                                         $58,066.40

In this example, the total monthly costs of the reservations and inquiries fall short of the $60,000 payroll. In addition perhaps the reservationists performed a third untracked activity like canceling tickets. A complication with the cycle-time output measure approach involves:

- Cost and time of the processor (the reservationist).
- The cycle time of the process/activity (reservation, inquiries).
- The quantity of the processes (reservations, inquiries).

The cost-load rates, average processing cycle-time rates, and total cost are usually determined during measurement periods that differ from the period for which costs are being accounted.

Correcting this situation is not a major issue. If a complete reconciliation with period expenditures is the goal, the cost rates can be modified upward or downward to force the complete reconciliation.

The percent approach to costing activities and outputs is simpler because it first apportions the total costs and then the cost driver rates. However, with the percent approach, processing cycle-time and potential capacity constraints cannot be measured or assessed. The cycle-time approach allows capacity planning and constraint-checking for process management. The percent approach is a *cost-push* technique whereas the cycle-time approach is a *demand-pull* technique. (Refer back to Section 4.3.)

7–9. ESTIMATING PURCHASED MATERIAL AND SERVICES COSTS

The attention thus far for data collection has been strictly on the employee-related time-effort expenditures (e.g., salary, fringe benefits, and so on). How do nonpayroll-related and purchased material expenditures from third parties get assigned from the general ledger into activities? As mentioned earlier, it is best to restrict these assigned costs to those activities already defined for what people and machines do. That is, do not create new activities (except for only a handful of inanimate enterprise-consuming activities like building rent or taxes).

In an ideal ABC/ABM world, the perfect place to capture purchased costs is as close as possible to the point of use at the time of consumption. For example, if a specific item like a perishable chemical is ordered for a specific application for a specific product, the pertinent activity code number could be recorded as early in time as possible and directly on the initial purchase order. If the purchased item is for stock for later use, the activity number could be coded on a material issue ticket when the item is subsequently consumed. This kind of record-keeping is virtually identical to that of a work order in a job shop or project accounting system. In effect, you are direct-charging the purchased item to its activity and to its intended final cost object.

But this is not an ideal world, and the discipline and extra effort to code material acquisition and issuance information that close to the point of use is likely not worth it. Ask yourself, "Is the climb worth the view?" A more economical alternative is to again rely on estimating techniques.

A practical estimating approach involves first isolating a Pareto ranking of roughly 90 percent of the non-wage related general ledger account balances for expenses (e.g., supplies, travel, etc.). Then assign the cost of the larger dollar accounts to one of three broad categories:

1. Direct charge to an activity (i.e., to within a business process).
2. An enterprisewide or infrastructure-sustaining activity.
3. Employee-related use and occupancy, called superfringe benefits.

These three costs assignment paths are shown in Figure 7–12.

For some ledger accounts, it may be worth the effort to retain the originating cost center or department identification rather than using the total, across-the-organization expense. However, often the purchasing location is not where the activity cost is incurred. Therefore, it may be simpler to first assign the entire account expenditures to one of the three aforementioned categories to disconnect the expense relationships from its cost center; and then apportion further from there, if necessary.

Here are further descriptions of the three expenditure categories:

1. *Direct charge to a business process activity.* Many purchased items or services can be naturally associated with the verb-adjective-noun activities already defined for people. They are simply consumed as employees do the work activity. For example, the cost for corrugated boxes is likely consumed when people pack material. In some cases, the purchased cost may be consumed by two or more activities located in proximity of one another. How do you distribute these costs among the multiple activities? Ok, fan it (i.e., arbitrarily allocate it, that dirty word) the best you can. The majority of diversity has already been reflected by isolating the activity cost, so a little estimation error is tolerable.

FIGURE 7-12

Estimating Purchased Items

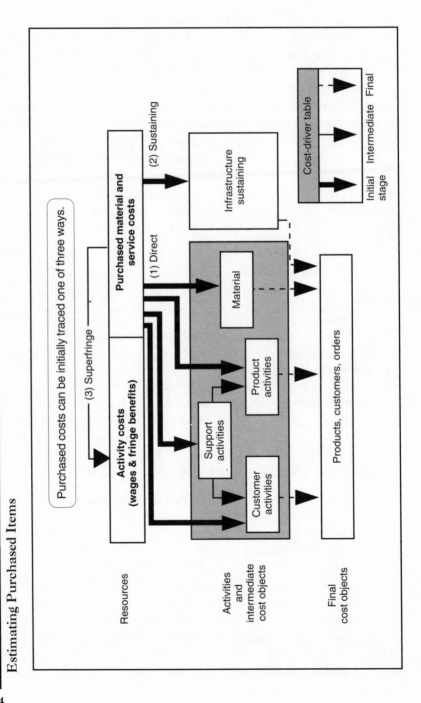

Purchased costs can be initially traced one of three ways.

Purchased material and service costs

Activity costs (wages & fringe benefits)

(1) Direct

(2) Sustaining

(3) Superfringe

Infrastructure sustaining

Material

Product activities

Support activities

Customer activities

Products, customers, orders

Cost-driver table

Initial stage   Intermediate   Final

Resources

Activities and intermediate cost objects

Final cost objects

2. *Enterprisewide sustaining activities.* Some purchased items or
   services like building rent, taxes, lawn-cutting services, or the
   company picnic are arguably not directly required by business
   processes or by their final cost objects. They are pure support
   costs or highly discretionary expenses. These expenses should
   be combined with the people-related infrastructure-sustaining
   activities. When full-absorption, fully burdened costing is
   absolutely required for decisions (or to satisfy Generally
   Accepted Accounting Practices, or GAAP, such as for inventory
   costing), segment the reporting for these overhead costs as a tax
   or surcharge to their cost objects (revisit Section 1–3).
3. *Employee use and occupancy.* Some purchases like office
   furniture, laptop computers, travel, and phone bills are highly
   correlated with the number of employees. These costs, once
   isolated, can simply be combined with cost of salaries and
   fringe benefits. In effect, these purchases are costs to support
   employees as resources, which is why they are called
   superfringe. These costs will then get baked into the activity
   costs via the employee wage-related assignment and estimating
   exercise described in Section 7–7.

Figure 7–13 integrates the relationship map with the labor and
third-party purchased primary material costs and reconciles the activity-
based view to a company's financial profit-and-loss statement. The suppliers' column reflects the major raw materials (excluding indirect purchases). In the company's column, the enterprise converts those materials
into products with its labor costs combined with the purchased consum-
ables at the level of an activity. These activity costs are then organized by
the core business processes defined by the relationship map. Note that
the enterprisewide infrastructure-sustaining costs (graph E) have been
segregated from the core business processes costs.

At this stage, all but roughly a small percentage of the remaining
nonwage expenses will have been translated from general ledger resource costs into activity costs. How should you assign the low-dollar remaining expenses? The easiest, most practical way is to combine these
with the employee use and occupancy costs, baking them all into activity
costs. Otherwise, selectively extract any individual ledger account cost
balances that you strongly feel are either directly chargeable to a business
process activity or are infrastructure-sustaining and combine the dollars
that are left with the employee superfringe use and occupancy dollars.

FIGURE 7–13

Reconciling Activity Cost with the Profit and Loss Report

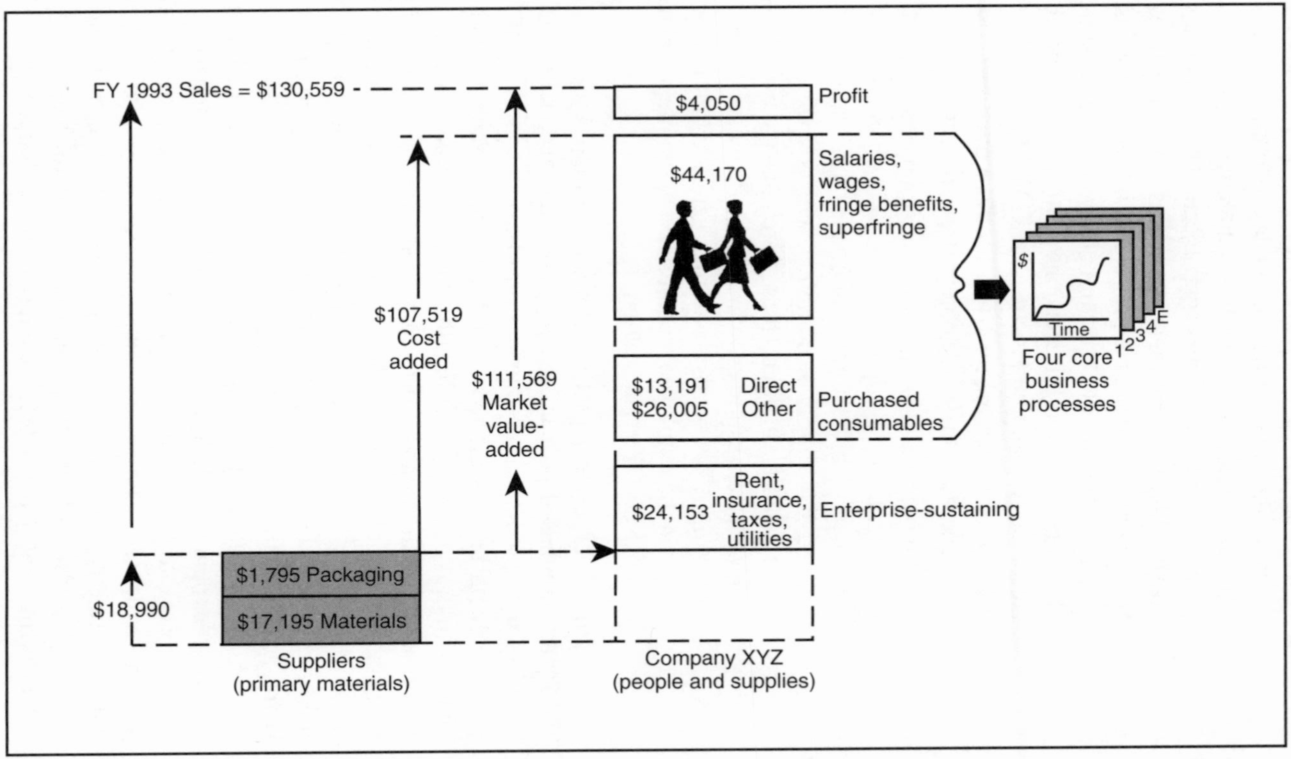

In summary, an increased magnitude of visibility (i.e., granularity) comes only from the expansion of the verb-adjective-noun activities at their lowest level; for example, going from about 75 activities for the high-altitude flyover to roughly 250 activities for the low-altitude flyby. Any improvement in the ABC/ABM model's accuracy comes either from (1) the expanded segmenting of activities if the same flyover functional representatives do the estimating or (2) the greater familiarity with employee work-time by enlisting additional estimators who are more likely to be more familiar with and closer to where work gets done by people.

What's the point of all of this? Getting management's attention regarding their core business processes by using ABM supply value-chain cost data is one accomplishment. However, structuring the data along and within processes to build strong and compelling business cases for action requires a lot more focus and analysis. In Section 7–12 we will discuss how ABM data can be used to stimulate management actions.

7–10. CONVERTING ABM INTO ABC: ASSIGNING ACTIVITY COSTS TO FINAL COST OBJECTS

This section describes how to use cost drivers to perform the product and service costing calculations. *Activity cost drivers are used to integrate the cost flow from activities to other activities and eventually to final cost objects.* Activity cost drivers can be defined as any event that causes a change in the consumption of an activity by other activities, products, suppliers, or customers. (Refer to Figure 7–14).

A way to identify an activity cost driver is to ask an employee who performs a specific activity, "What would make the magnitude of your time spent on your activity appreciably go up or go down?" For example, the activity "process invoices" would have the number of invoices as its activity cost driver. Figure 7–15 expands on how to identify activity cost drivers. Cost drivers should ideally be discretely measurable in quantity (to determine the activity cost rate) and traceable to unique cost objects (e.g., as "the processed invoices" would be to individual customers).

In sum, an activity cost driver measures the frequency and intensity of the demands placed on activities by cost objects, as illustrated in Figure 7–16. They are individually variable and can best explain the behavior of an activity cost.

FIGURE 7 - 1 4

Defining Activity Cost Drivers

Activity cost drivers explain why activities are performed.

Two-stage ABC model

Resources

Resource and
intermediate
cost drivers

Activities

Output
cost rates

Final
activity
cost
drivers

Final
cost objects

Defenition:

Activity cost drivers are any event that
causes a change in the consumption of
activity. They are the factors that govern
the work load and effort required to
perform an activity.

- Final activity cost drivers link the cumulative
  costs of upstream activities with the final
  product or customer.

- All activity cost drivers (including
  intermediates) reflect cause-and-effect
  relationships.

- Activity cost drivers trace and reassign
  activity costs to their cost objects in direct
  proportion to the objects' consumption of
  the activity.

FIGURE 7 - 1 5

Identifying Activity Cost Drivers

To identify activity cost drivers, *ask:*

- What causes differences in the level of
  effort in the activity?
- Why do we do this activity (i.e., what's the
  root cause)?

 Activity cost drivers carry "sending" data to cost objects, which
answers "to whom and how much of me?"

FIGURE 7-16

Visualizing Cost Driver Consumptions

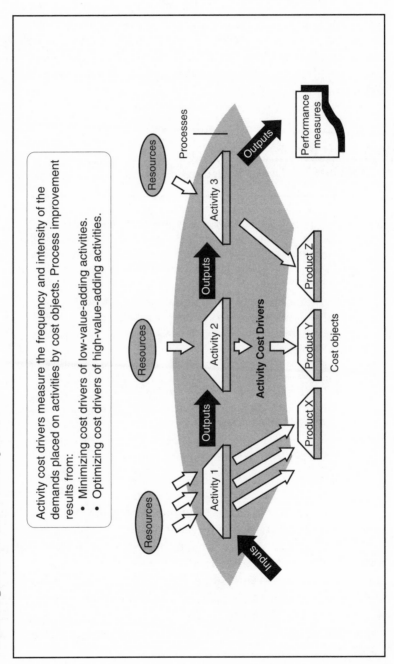

Straightforward guidelines for selecting activity cost drivers are described in Figure 7–17. It is important to restrict the number of activity cost drivers to a manageable few while always testing the trade-offs between the effort to collect extra data, accuracy, and the amount of precision the end-user needs for decision making. Remember to ask, "Is the climb worth the view?"

FIGURE   7–17

Activity Cost Driver Selection Guidelines

Selecting each activity cost driver is tricky because it must be quantifiable and link each of the individual cost objects to the upstream activity or activities the cost object causes to exist. Guidelines for choosing them include:

■ Avoid activity cost drivers for immaterial activity costs.
■ Pick activity cost drivers that match the type of activity.
■ Pick drivers that have a high correlation to the actual consumption rate of its activity.
■ Minimize the number of unique activity cost drivers because there will be diminishing returns in accuracy.
■ Find activity drivers that encourage performance improvements.
■ Pick activity drivers that are economical to measure, and avoid activity drivers that require new methods of measurement.

Source: Angela Norkiewicz, Manager, Cost, Pennsylvania Blue Shield.

Figure 7–18 provides a sampling of popular product-related and customer-related activity cost drivers.

Inexperienced ABC designers believe their models will require hundreds of intermediate and final activity cost drivers that are electronically interfaced to feeder systems. They fail to appreciate that simply increasing the number of activities to segment cost diversity alleviates the need for the cost drivers to reflect the diversity. Figure 7–19 shows a continuum of activity cost drivers that trades off reduced accuracy for reduced effort to collect the data.

FIGURE 7-18

Examples of Activity Cost Drivers

Examples of activity cost drivers are below. Each driver must answer, "To whom and how much?"

Product-Related Cost Drivers	Customer-Related Cost Drivers
■ # of machine hours by product	■ # of complaints
■ # of purchase orders	■ # of customers
■ # of line items per PO	■ # of sales calls
■ # of inspections	■ # of line items picked
■ # of ingredients	■ # of trucks shipped
■ # of work orders	■ # of customer orders
■ # of material movements	■ # of order changes
■ # of receipts	■ # of private-label products

A sound approach to leveraging activity cost drivers is to phase in the level of sophistication. This means first listing an ideal cost driver for each activity, then reasonably selecting far few drivers covering several activities, but relying on functional representatives to manually estimate the 100 percent mix to the next downstream cost objects. Beyond that, as warranted, the ABC/ABM system maintainers can over time selectively replace those drivers with more responsive and accurate volume-sensitive transaction drivers from feeder systems.

7–11. BUSINESS PROCESS VISUALIZATION— GRAPHICALLY PRESENTING COSTS WITHIN CORE PROCESSES

An excellent way to present business process value-chain cost data is graphically; an optional support is to provide numerical data in tables. Many end-users, particularly senior executives, are not clear about exactly what a business process is or looks like. Remember, they have been saturated for years with cost data related to the organization chart, not the processes. From a graph or picture, end-users visualize a business

FIGURE 7-19

Ladder of Activity-Cost Driver Assignment Techniques

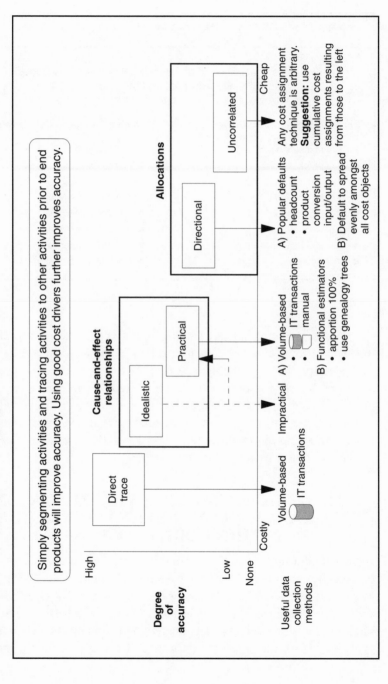

process as something physical and real. Remember, a process is an arterial network of two or more activities, each conforming to verb-adjective-noun grammar; and a process is customer-directed. That verb part of each activity description represents the consumption of costs.

Figure 7–20 shows data reflecting a manufacturing company's annual work-effort activities of 4,200 full-time equivalents (FTEs), employees who were defined and estimated by functional estimators. The

FIGURE 7-20

Five XYZ Company Activity Cost Spreadsheets

ID #	Process Name / Task Name	Lead Time (Days)	Process %	Task % Split	FTE	$	Consum	Fac Sust	Raw Matl	Contr	Total Purch $	Total $
				Heads: 100		$/FTE: $35,000						
1010	**Process customer RFQ**		10%									
1010.1	Assign RFQ number	1		20%	2.0	$70,000	2.0%	2.0%			$470,056	$540,056
1010.2	Qualify/validate RFQ	5			0.0	$0	0.0%	0.0%			$0	$0
1010.3	Distribute RFQ documentation	3			0.0	$0	0.0%	0.0%			$0	$0
1010.4	Prepare RFQ response	15		80%	8.0	$280,000	8.0%	8.0%			$1,880,225	$2,160,225
1010.5	Get customer approval and PO	30			0.0	$0	0.0%	0.0%			$0	$0
1020	**Process customer order**		0%									
1020.1	Assign order number	2			0.0	$0	0.0%	0.0%			$0	$0
1020.2	Validate order information	4			0.0	$0	0.0%	0.0%			$0	$0
1020.3	Communicate with customer	5			0.0	$0	0.0%	0.0%			$0	$0
1020.4	Enter order in order system	1			0.0	$0	0.0%	0.0%			$0	$0
1020.5	Send order to Product Engineering	2			0.0	$0	0.0%	0.0%			$0	$0
1030	**Design product**		10%									
1030.1	Analyze requirements	15			0.0	$0	0.0%	0.0%			$0	$0
1030.2	Convert reqts into design specifications	15			0.0	$0	0.0%	0.0%			$0	$0
1030.3	Create engineering design prints	10			0.0	$0	0.0%	0.0%			$0	$0
1030.4	Create tooling print package	10			0.0	$0	0.0%	0.0%			$0	$0
1030.5	Approve design/tooling print packages	10		100%	10.0	$350,000	10.0%	10.0%			$2,350,281	$2,700,281
1030.6	Archive design documentation	15			0.0	$0	0.0%	0.0%			$0	$0
1030.7	Approve print packages	15			0.0	$0	0.0%	0.0%			$0	$0
1030.8	Release print packages	3			0.0	$0	0.0%	0.0%			$0	$0
1030.9	Get customer design approval	10			0.0	$0	0.0%	0.0%			$0	$0
1040	**Process engineering change orders**		10%									
1040.1	Receive request for change	1			0.0	$0	0.0%	0.0%			$0	$0
1040.2	Document problem and change required	5		20%	2.0	$70,000	2.0%	2.0%			$470,056	$540,056
1040.3	Create solution documentation	15		80%	8.0	$280,000	8.0%	8.0%			$1,880,225	$2,160,225
1040.4	Approve print package	3			0.0	$0	0.0%	0.0%			$0	$0
1040.5	Release print package	1			0.0	$0	0.0%	0.0%			$0	$0
1040.6	Get customer/requester approval	5			0.0	$0	0.0%	0.0%			$0	$0
1040.7	Schedule implementation	3			0.0	$0	0.0%	0.0%			$0	$0
1040.8	Implement change	25			0.0	$0	0.0%	0.0%			$0	$0
1050	**Plan/schedule production**		5%									
1050.1	Review and approve print package	5			0.0	$0	0.0%	0.0%			$0	$0
1050.2	Assign cost tracking number	1		100%	5.0	$175,000	5.0%	5.0%			$1,175,141	$1,350,141
1050.3	Plan process routing	2			0.0	$0	0.0%	0.0%			$0	$0
1050.4	Assign manpower	3			0.0	$0	0.0%	0.0%			$0	$0
1050.5	Set and release Job Plan	1			0.0	$0	0.0%	0.0%			$0	$0
1050.6	Expedite orders	2			0.0	$0	0.0%	0.0%			$0	$0
1060	**Procure materials**		20%									
1060.1	Select vendors	20		60%	12.0	$420,000	12.0%	12.0%			$2,820,337	$3,240,337
1060.2	Issue POs	5		20%	4.0	$140,000	4.0%	4.0%			$940,112	$1,080,112
1060.3	Receive materials	20			0.0	$0	0.0%	0.0%			$0	$0
1060.4	Pay vendors	0		20%	4.0	$140,000	4.0%	4.0%			$940,112	$1,080,112
1070	**Manufacture product**		0%									
1070.1	Transfer drawings to English meas.	2			0.0	$0	0.0%	0.0%			$0	$0
1070.2	Set machine and change dies	2			0.0	$0	0.0%	0.0%			$0	$0
1070.3	Manufacture parts	8			0.0	$0	0.0%	0.0%			$0	$0
1070.4	Assemble parts	4			0.0	$0	0.0%	0.0%			$0	$0
1070.5	Inspect and test assemblies	2			0.0	$0	0.0%	0.0%			$0	$0
1070.6	Update cost tracking system	1			0.0	$0	0.0%	0.0%			$0	$0
1070.7	Identify and resolve problems	10			0.0	$0	0.0%	0.0%			$0	$0
1080	**Deliver product**		20%									
1080.1	Create shipping documents	1			0.0	$0	0.0%	0.0%			$0	$0
1080.2	Inspect completed order	0.5			0.0	$0	0.0%	0.0%			$0	$0
1080.3	Package product	0.2			0.0	$0	0.0%	0.0%			$0	$0
1080.4	Ship product to customer	4.5			0.0	$0	0.0%	0.0%			$0	$0
1080.5	Update order system	1			0.0	$0	0.0%	0.0%			$0	$0
1080.6	Invoice customer	15		75%	15.0	$525,000	15.0%	15.0%			$3,525,422	$4,050,422
1080.7	Receive payment	30		25%	5.0	$175,000	5.0%	5.0%			$1,175,141	$1,350,141
1090	**Maintain assets**		0%									
1090.1	Maintain equipment	0			0.0	$0	0.0%	0.0%			$0	$0
1090.2	Maintain facilities	0			0.0	$0	0.0%	0.0%			$0	$0
1100	**Support primary business processes**		25%									
1100.1	HR, MIS, Accounting, Admin., etc.	0		100%	25.0	$875,000	25.0%	25.0%			$5,875,703	$6,750,703
Totals		369.2	100%		100	3,5000,000	100%	100%			23,502,810	27,002,810

Dept 105–Personnel
Dept 104–Sales and Marketing
Dept 103–Engineering
Dept 102–Manufacturing
Dept 101–Financial

activities reflect a subset of the company's 6,102 total employees. The quantified activity costs are for only those that run across the specific business process of "from inquiry to customer delivery," which is one of the company's four core business processes. (Therefore, 1,902 other FTEs are accounted for in three similar business processes.) This manufacturer's products are predominantly engineered to each customer's order. In this example, the activities comprising this specific "order fulfillment" process are mainly sequential.

As the costs of individual activities are accumulated, they chronologically produce the ABM cost build-up "mountain" graph in Figure 7–21. (This is where activities have been strung like pearls.) For this company's employees and managers, this experience was likely the first time they had visualized their collective efforts as a unified, measurable business process.

The vertical axis of the graph measures the cumulative cost build-up of the business process. The horizontal axis measures the cumulative cycle-time moving through the business process from start to finish for the product produced and all associated services.

As further background about this manufacturer, the annual costs of this order fulfillment process is $221,250,000. The employees produce about 100 end-items a year, averaging about two complete manufactured and assembled products per week. Each individual product, however, requires about a year, or 369 calendar days, to complete the core business process from beginning to end. (In practice, it doesn't matter if a company produces 100 or 1 million items in one year, one week, or one day.)

To help interpret this cumulative cost-added build-up graph, the final data point at the top-right corner represents the total annual enterprisewide costs consumed within the order fulfillment process. The vertical axis measures cumulative costs being consumed, while the horizontal axis reflects when costs are being incurred as time passes.

Do not confuse added costs with added value. Soon I'll discuss scoring of these added costs for value-added content. But for now, the focus is on costs only.

The slope of the curve between any two points is a tremendous attention director. A steep slope is potentially good because cost is rapidly being added. A flat slope is potentially bad because it implies time is passing while little or no costs are being added after the investment of capital has already begun. A flat slope indicates potentially low financial

FIGURE 7 - 21

XYZ Company Cost Build-Up Graphics

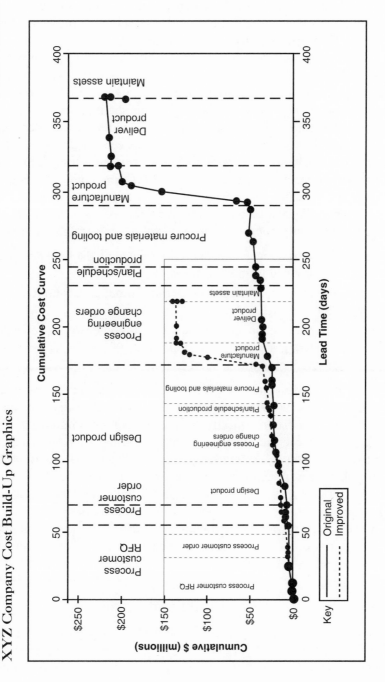

payback or rate of return. Note that I used the word *potentially* because steep slopes can include substantial non-value-adding costs and conversely flat slopes may have a reasonable explanation.

The average slope of the curve across the entire graph is $52,680 per FTE per year ($221,250,000 divided by 4,200 FTE employees). This slope serves as a composite baseline from which to compare other industry competitors (if that data is shared within the industry). However, it is apparent that the actual slopes between two points (or a cluster of points) can swing from steep to flat and back to steep. In this way, the graph serves primarily as a diagnostic tool that the organization can use to identify improvement opportunities. The slope at any point reflects the varying rate of financial return within the business process.

Figure 7–21 also presents a graph line of the process after it has been significantly improved. The observations are straightforward:

- The total annual domain process, noted by the final data point, has dropped from $221 million to $141 million.
- The cycle time to produce a typical product has shortened from 369 days to 225 days.
- The average slope of the curve has become steeper, reflecting an acceleration in cost being added ($95,000 per FTE per year based on a reduction from 4,200 to 1,484 FTEs).

Stockholders and chief financial officers like the second graph line because it reflects faster turnover of cash flow at the same time that labor productivity and, consequently, the profit margin has improved. The selling price for each product (i.e., annual revenues) has not changed because the products are market-priced; not necessarily derived from a cost-plus markup. Thus, profits must have increased. Process improvement teams also like the graph because it links the quantification of the potential cost savings to the detailed specific activities. Other investment or spending justification techniques are flawed by the assumptions of overhead allocations or narrow incremental analysis, which masks hidden costs elsewhere in the organization and business system.

Value Content in Processes

As earlier noted, a steep slope of the ABM cost build-up curve was *potentially* good. One should be cautious to declare a steep slope as unarguably good because there are always relative activities that employees and managers can describe and rank from "very desirable" to "nondesir-able." That is, some activities are value-adding and some are not—and activities, regardless of the amount of their cost, can be scored or graded along a value-added continuum from "very high" to "very low." (Revisit Section 4–5 for discussion on attributes and grading activities.)

The concept to understand here is that at points along the ABM cost build-up curve, the value-creating cost content of activities is usually a blend. And just having a steep slope does not prevent a range of costs from having a contaminated mix of high and low value-adding activities. Low value-adding activities are a target for waste elimination. Figure 7–22 shows an ABM cost build-up curve with the value-creating cost content layered, with the least desirable costs on the top layer. By imag-ining the complete delayering of the cost build-up curve, it is easier for employees to visualize where costs can potentially be reduced by elimi-nating low-value activities—and with the graph they can quantitatively measure by how much.

When ABM Cost Build-Up Graphs Don't Work

Some work environments are not so neatly made up of long, straight ser-ial business processes comprised of sequential activities (that is, the pearls do not string in a straight line). An advertising agency, for exam-ple, would be described by some as a reactive and chaotic workplace without any apparent manageable processes. Alternatively a personnel department or an airline reservations office may have individuals who each perform self-contained business processes. For workplaces where an ABM cost build-up curve simply does not apply, a much better visual and graphical presentation is that of a three-dimensional (3D) process flow network.

Figure 7–23 shows a 3D cost topography of a business process. In the figure's plane, the process flows are lying flat. The heights of the stacked columns represent the resource consumption costs per each ac-tivity (or summation of multiple activities). Similar to when using rela-tionship maps, the level of detail and granularity of process flow charts should be decomposed only down to an intermediate level—that sweet spot. That is, they should not be so complex as to turn off the audience, and not so simple as to not be stimulating and compelling to act on.

This 3D cost topography is what the high-altitude flyover and low-altitude flyby described earlier will show below the cloud cover. The

FIGURE 7-22

Process Cost Build-Up versus Time

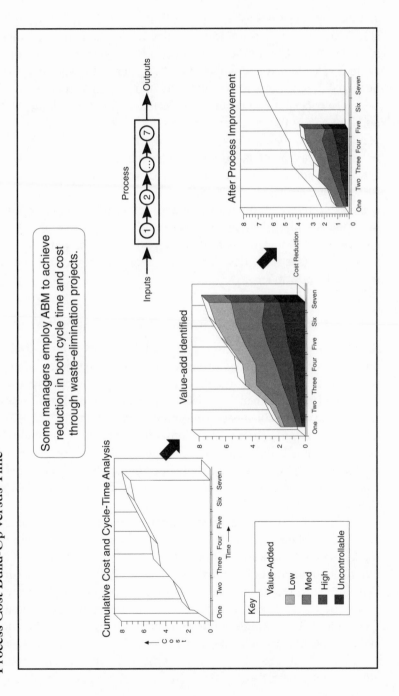

FIGURE 7-23

Visualizing Business Process Costs

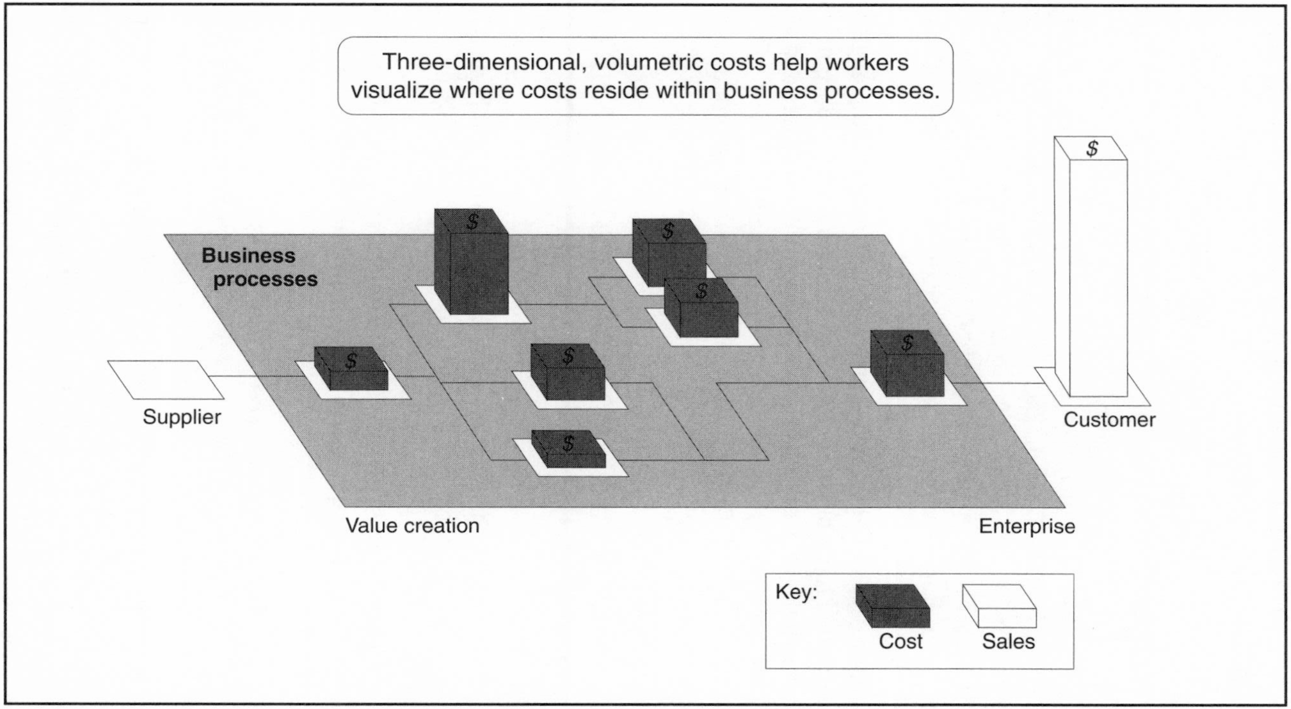

Three-dimensional, volumetric costs help workers visualize where costs reside within business processes.

Customer

Enterprise

Key:
Sales
Cost

Business processes

Value creation

Supplier

cubic volume of the stacked columns represents the total period cost in the time snapshot. And the total costs reconcile with the period's financial profit-and-loss statement.

Figure 7–24 visually shows the collection of activity cost stacks. Since sales exceed costs, the profit stack is also revealed.

Figure 7–25 shows the same 3D cost topography with the non-value-added costs highlighted.

Figure 7–26 diagrams how relationships between activities within complex business systems can be both related to each other and decomposed for greater detail (the cost stacks have not been shown). ABM costs can be assigned to the components of processes and visualized at any level. Some companies are already displaying these 3D costs to business improvement teams. With point-and-click drop-box and drag-down computer technology, teams can rapidly explore a wide range of information about their business processes, including which employees contribute to which work activities and what their skill sets and work-related experiences are. This kind of information becomes more critical as work content and work flow gets restructured to improve productivity and customer satisfaction.

7–12. ANALYZING COSTS FOR INSIGHTS (ROOT CAUSE ANALYSIS)

ABC/ABM data have previously been mentioned as a means to an end, where the end is the decision made and actions taken. Figure 7–27 shows a high-level view of how data is transformed with tools and analysis into results.

Figure 7–28 shows the four major flow paths with which the ABM data (as initially captured from labor and third-party purchases) can be analyzed:

1. Business process cost visibility—new views as to where the costs accumulate in the business process and at what rates.

2. Business process change impact cost/benefit analysis
   - Capabilities to score or grade the value content of work and resource consumption.
   - Ability to quantify the work and the costs that may go away with changes.

Visualizing Business Process Costs

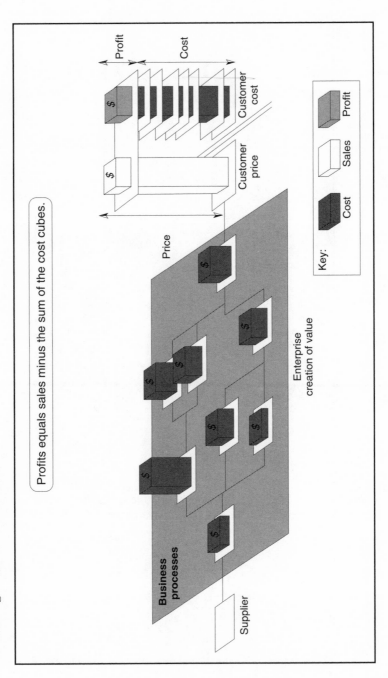

Profits equals sales minus the sum of the cost cubes.

FIGURE 7-25

Visualizing Non-Value-Adding Costs

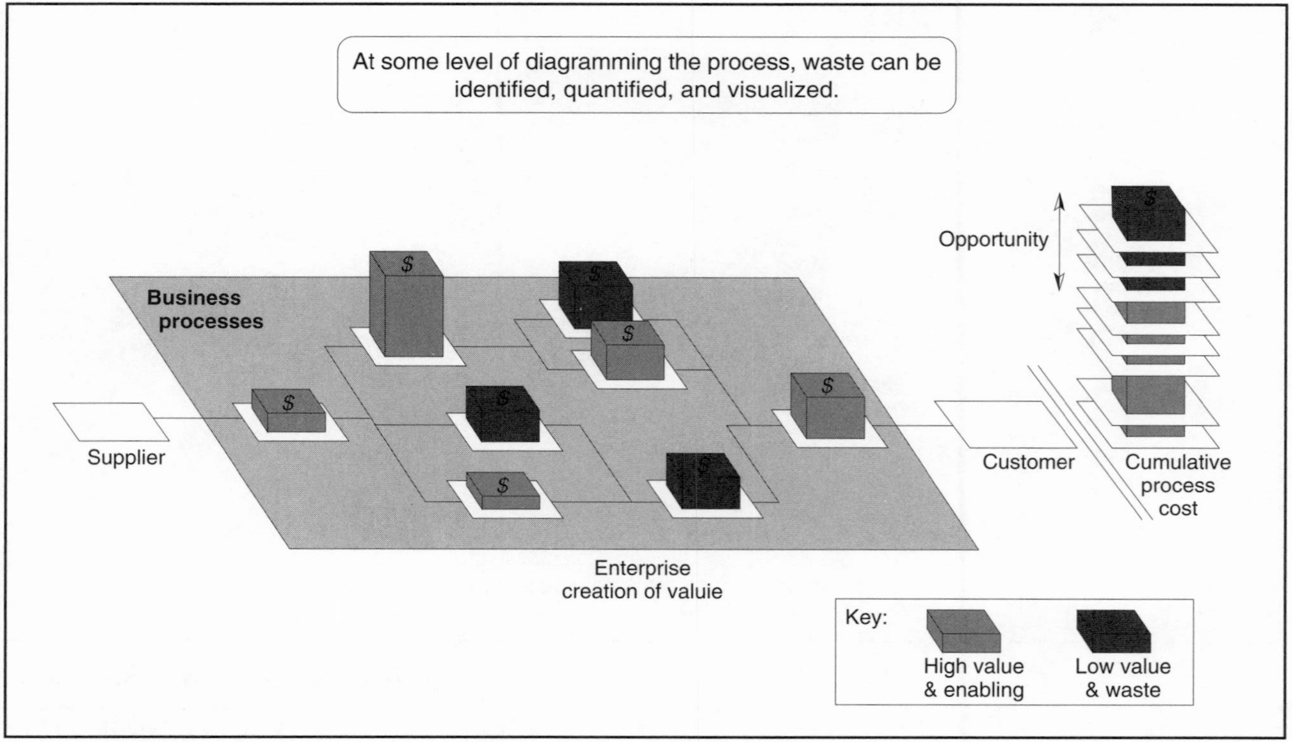
At some level of diagramming the process, waste can be identified, quantified, and visualized.
Business processes
$
Supplier
Enterprise creation of valuie
Customer
Opportunity
Cumulative process cost
Key:
High value & enabling
Low value & waste

FIGURE 7 - 2 6

Decomposing Processes to Increase Granularity

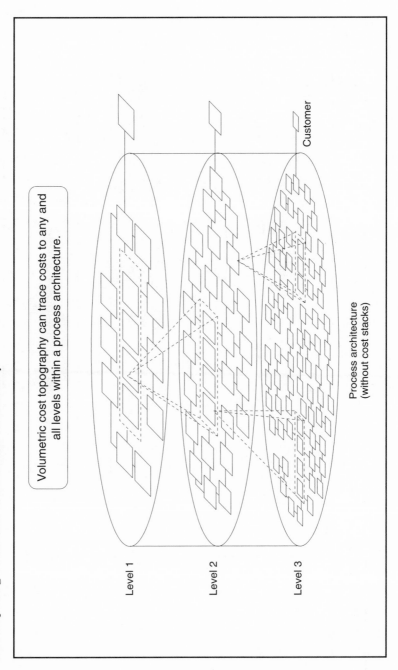

Volumetric cost topography can trace costs to any and all levels within a process architecture.

Level 1

Level 2

Level 3

Customer

Process architecture
(without cost stacks)

FIGURE 7–27

Using the Data

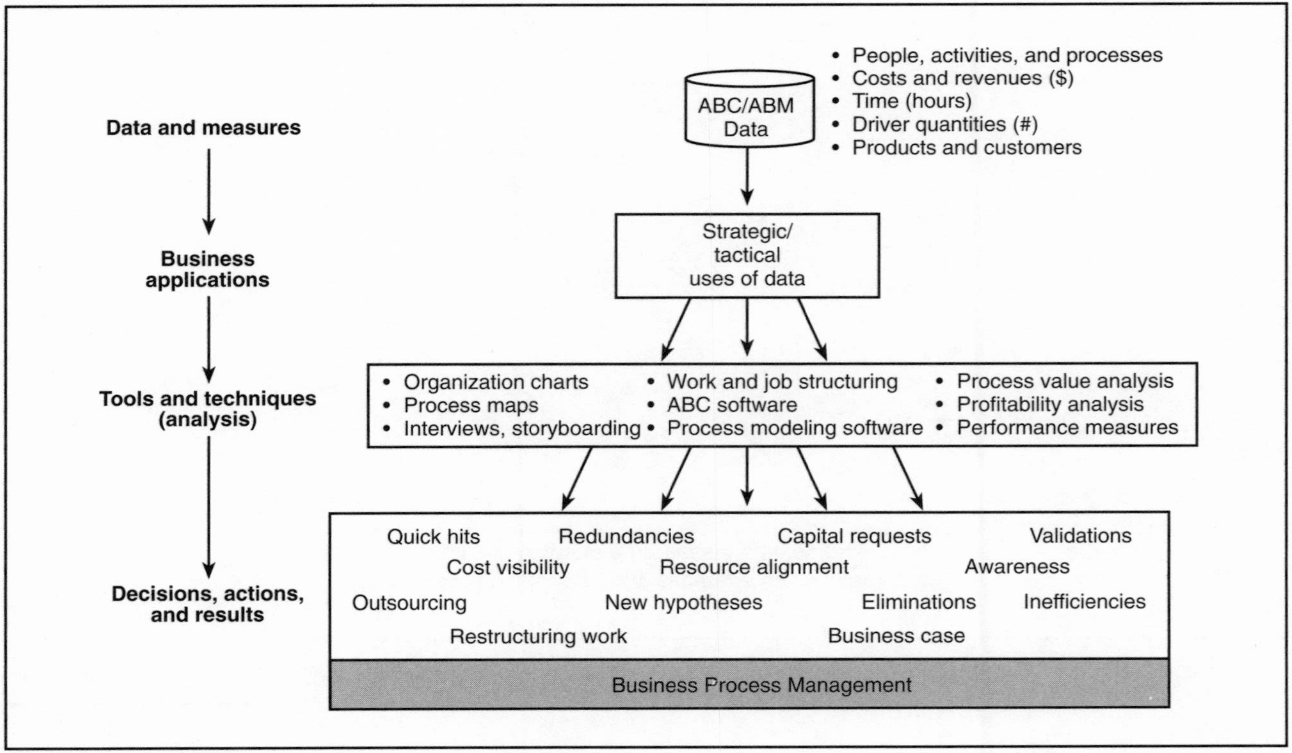

- People, activities, and processes
- Costs and revenues ($)
- Time (hours)
- Driver quantities (#)
- Products and customers

Data and measures

ABC/ABM Data

Business applications

Strategic/tactical uses of data

Tools and techniques (analysis)

- Organization charts
- Process maps
- Interviews, storyboarding
- Work and job structuring
- ABC software
- Process modeling software
- Process value analysis
- Profitability analysis
- Performance measures

Decisions, actions, and results

Quick hits   Redundancies   Capital requests   Validations

Cost visibility   Resource alignment   Awareness

Outsourcing   New hypotheses   Eliminations   Inefficiencies

Restructuring work   Business case

Business Process Management

FIGURE 7-28

From Data to Analysis to Action (Detail)

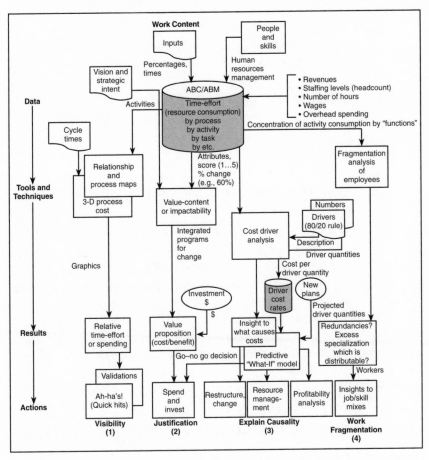

3. Root cost analysis
   - Identification of cost drivers and their magnitudes to determine what causes work and costs to occur.
   - These cost relationships are also used for product and customer profitability analysis, activity-based budgeting, product and service line costing, and what-if scenario planning.
4. Worker fragmentation analysis—How is the mix of work either concentrated or widely distributed among employees?
   - If too concentrated, the work may be dispersed to existing employees.
   - If too widely distributed, there may be excess redundancy and overlap, which can be consolidated among fewer employees.

Although all four broad uses of the ABC/ABM data are of great value, root cause analysis may well be the best. By definition *causes* reflect the reasons an activity exists, whereas *effects* describe the activity after the cause. ABC/ABM data reveal more effect than cause. In other words, costs are really symptoms of more deep-seated processes.

Figure 7–29 shows an example of one kind of root-cause diagramming technique. Fishbone diagrams are an alternative technique. Both are popular brainstorming techniques that employees can use to analyze and understand what and where to change things for the better.

ABC/ABM data serves as an enabler to bring focus, not as a solution.

7–13. WHERE DOES ABM DATA FIT INTO THIS?

Process-based thinking is infectious and will likely be long-lived. But for this decade, business processes will likely fade in and out of managers' and employees' thinking, temporarily displaced by deadlines, misaligned reward systems, departmental crises, and other distractions—regardless of any dainty relationship maps and process flow charts. ABM's contribution is its ability to quantify and place measurable cost data into these diagrams. ABM can make the accounting data a great attention-getter and reinforcer to influence people to think process not function.

In short, ABM populates cross-functional business processes and supply value-chains with their consumed activity costs. These costs reinforce managers' and employees' thinking that the business process will

FIGURE 7-29

Activity Costs Measure More Effect Than Cause

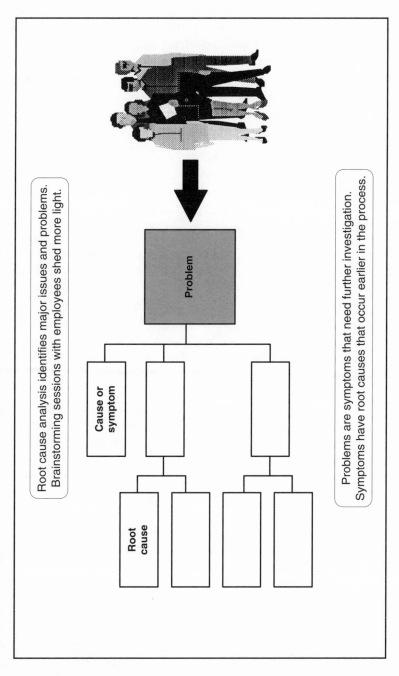

always be there regardless of the organization chart. *ABM data can help operationalize process-based thinking.* No other metric can do that as effectively. Quality data and cycle-time data, though valuable to specific teams and individuals, are too fungible to reinforce core business process thinking. But resource cost consumption data, when stated financially, is another matter. ABM cost data:

- Is expressed in monetary terms, the universal language of business.
- Is a common denominator, a unit-of-measure conversion of how an enterprise spends time and energy in reacting to unplanned occurrences and how it behaves in general.
- Links directly to profit-and-loss statements, the official and institutional company report cards of choice.

ABM is the ultimate in direct costing because it does so for the total enterprise. Cost drivers, not uncorrelated allocations, provide the cause-and-effect linkages. Don't be persuaded by managers advocating improvement programs in which "costs will take care of themselves" without capturing cost measurements—both before and after the improvement program on an enterprisewide basis. Use cost measurements in conjunction with TQM, JIT, and any other process redesign programs.

> If organizations' management accounting systems fail to provide useful signals for measuring the efficiency of processes and profitability of products, the ability of senior executives to manager their large enterprises will diminish.
>
> *H. Thomas Johnson and Robert S. Kaplan*[2]

---

2. H. Thomas Johnson and Robert S. Kaplan, *Relevance Lost: The Rise and Fall of Management Accounting* (Boston, MA: Harvard Business School Press, 1987), p. 260.

CHAPTER 8

Common Misconceptions about ABC/ABM

The goal of a good product cost system should be to make more obvious, more transparent, how costs currently considered to be fixed or sunk actually do vary with decisions made about product output, product mix, and product diversity.

H. Thomas Johnson and Robert S. Kaplan[1]

Earlier in this book, I discussed why some ABC/ABM implementations fail. Many of those reasons involved misconceptions about what an ABC/ABM project requires. Routine misconceptions involve (1) the amount and detail level of data, (2) the degree of accuracy of costs, (3) the length of time needed to define activities and collect data, (4) the dilemma of having two sets of books, and (5) the necessity to select and purchase specialized ABC software. Each misconception will now be discussed.

8–1. DATA: HOW MUCH? HOW DETAILED?

Many believe that ABC/ABM involves a ton of hard work with a mudslide of data waiting to bury everybody, particularly the accountants. In reality, ABC/ABM models can be of a manageable size. The level of detail depends on the kinds of decisions made with the new data.

ABC/ABM models are rarely elaborate or finely granular. Pareto's 80/20 law of diminishing returns is heavily deployed in the design and construction of ABC/ABM models (i.e., 80 percent of what matters is explainable by a concentrated 20 percent of what's happening). ABC/ABM models simply provide visibility that is missing from traditional systems. They accomplish this by using an activity-based philosophy with verb-adjective-noun grammar. When the outdated, function-based philosophy

---

1. H. Thomas Johnson and Robert S. Kaplan, *Relevance Lost: The Rise and Fall of Management Accounting* (Boston, MA: Harvard Business School Press, 1987), p. 235.

FIGURE 8-1

Five Misconceptions

Common ABC misconceptions	
Misconception	**Reality**
■ ABC requires a massive amount of data and detail, plus tremendous maintenance.	■ The level of detail, accuracy, and frequency of reporting depends on the kinds of decisions the data are used for.
■ ABC data must be very accurate.	■ It is better to be approximately correct than precisely inaccurate.
■ It is tremendous work to collect a mudslide of data.	■ Pareto's 80/20 rule allows for significant amounts of estimation from informed participants within a business process, combined with a few key interfaces to operational databases.
■ ABC creates a separate set of financial books, which leads to confusion.	■ Management can guide users as to which set of books to use. With time, companies will integrate their general ledger with their activity accounting system.
■ You can not do ABC without special ABC software.	■ The initial learning process can use spreadsheet software to translate financial ledger data into activities. However, cost flows into interim cost objects requires network-based ABC software.

is followed, such as in models that use vertical organization chart structures with chart-of-accounts language, then massive, detailed reporting is often deployed instead of relevance. Put the data on a diet!

The best advice concerning the amount of data and level of detail is to design the system for decision makers' needs. If the model is too simple, it won't be sufficiently accurate; but if it is too complicated, the extra effort to maintain it may exceed the benefits. Understand the trade-offs between the relevance, significance, accuracy, and flexibility required to capture the diversity of resource consumption at timely intervals. The process view (ABM) involves visibility for directing attention, so some amount of error is tolerable. The final cost object view (ABC) requires relatively more accuracy than ABM.

8–2. HOW ACCURATE MUST THE ABC/ABM DATA BE?

As for the previous issue, the answer to this question depends on the kind of decisions being made with the new data. In most cases, informed estimates are as good as direct measurements and intense calculations. For the process view (ABM), the data is usually used to create visibility and for attention-directing purposes, so there is moderate tolerance for error. An ABM model can decompose activities without any distortion. In contrast, for the final cost object view (ABC) accuracy becomes the primary issue.

If management's strategic intent is to understand sources of profit by products, services, channels, and market segments, there is room for some error, but substantially less error than with ABM. Comparing the new results to those found with a traditional allocation approach, you'll find enormous undercosted and overcosted error differences. Always remember Professor Robert Kaplan's now famous ABC observation: "It is better to be approximately correct than precisely inaccurate."

For ABC, if management's intent is more tactical than strategic, such as for individual price quotations at the customer-order level, then a greater effort with more cost drivers and more segmented activities may be necessary to detect diversity's impact on resource cost consumption. ABC's cost flows to cost objects cannot be scaled downward, unlike the cost flow of resources directly to activities, because diversity is captured and simultaneously redistributed at each cost flow stage. Again, remember to follow Pareto's 80-20 rule.

8–3. HOW CAN ACTIVITY DATA BE QUICKLY BUT EFFECTIVELY COLLECTED?

Many believe it takes forever to construct a chart of activities and then collect the time and spending data from employees. Further, they believe the outputs will be tainted with estimating errors and therefore unreliable. These beliefs are false. For starters, by first having high-level process flow charts created by cross-functional teams, probably 90 percent of the activities will already have been defined by informed people who have a stake in the business' success. The activity dictionary can be dropped down in resolution one additional level in the process architecture by simply soliciting a few (two to five) verb-noun activities of work content within each step of the process flow chart. This data collection technique employs a top-down approach.

If high-level process maps do not exist, an alternative top-down data collection method is to ask each functional department (stovepipe) to list the 5 to 10 significant activities that take up the time of employees within their function. A helpful tip is for them to consider their function's outputs to remind them of their activities.

With ABC, closeness is much better than precision; therefore, only a handful of close-to-the-process middle managers (i.e., functional estimators) are needed for estimating what percent of time natural work groups of people doing similar work are apportioned to the already-defined activities. In a few days, the data can be crunched using your favorite spreadsheet software. Collecting non-wage-related expenses, like utilities or supplies, goes just as fast. (See Section 7–6.)

8–4. TWO SETS OF BOOKS?

Many believe ABC can replace their traditional general-ledger-based accounting system. No, ABC is a translator inserted to extract general ledger and other data; it is used like a corrective optical lens to bring clarity. The general ledger collects a blizzard of transactions and serves as an accumulator. ABC translates that raw and arguably unusable data. Remember, ABC is a form of a direct cost accounting of largely indirect costs. It uses surrogate cost drivers for those costs normally not thought of as directly making end products or services.

ABC is, at least initially, an off-line complement that interfaces to existing data systems. After ABC is better understood, users usually simplify their routine accounting procedures used to satisfy regulatory requirements (e.g., GAAP reporting for inventories). They then link their new activity-based data to managerial reports to provide better decision-making capability, instruct employees to no longer use the regulatory accounting data, and finally stop perpetuating decisions based on the old, flawed data. Advanced and mature users are moving toward fully integrated, permanent ABC production systems. However, that step requires a good information systems plan, as well as buy-in from the end-users.

8-5. IS SPECIALIZED ABC/ABM SOFTWARE NECESSARY?

Many believe special ABC software is initially required. PC-based or client-server ABC/ABM software becomes necessary when users have needs for multistage cost flows and want to take the optional next step beyond converting general ledger expenses into first-level activities. With PC-based ABC software, you can more conveniently convert those interactivity dollars into costs of other downstream activities, objects (e.g., parts, products, or customers), or outputs of processes (e.g., engineering changes). Without ABC/ABM software, you will hit the wall with spreadsheet software that is limited to two stages of cost flows.

Since ABC computations are primarily designed to segment the diversity of resource consumption, the activities that are costed do not necessarily need to be sequenced or mapped to a start-to-end process flow network. Some ABC/ABM software packages, however, combine the process flow functionality with the ABC cost flow segmenting. Other ABC/ABM software vendors have established relationships with process-modeling and data analysis software vendors, sharing data.

Many companies are initially content to simply convert general ledger expenses into cross-functional processes comprised of activities. This initial step can be done using your favorite spreadsheet software. If you desire the optional next step—product costing or more elaborate process modeling—most ABC/ABM software will accept downloads of data from spreadsheet software. In addition, activity cost driver data, like batch-related equipment changeovers, which further distributes activity costs according to unique consumption patterns, can be downloaded from production-based computer systems.

Beyond the basic ABC software functionality, other more advanced software features include:

- Multiple ABC model construction with consolidation of multiple models into a single larger model.
- Single ABC model construction, but capability for two or more users to independently modify different parts of the model for subsequent merging.
- Substantial (virtually unlimited) model size to allow large numbers of activities, cost assignment paths, cost drivers, attributes, cost objects, and resources. Attributes should be capable of being attached at the lowest activity level and uniquely flow through any consolidation roll-ups.

- Multiple period reporting for trend analysis and historical improvement program benefits realization analysis.
- Flexible multilevel (arterial nodal) cost path flow to allow decomposing or aggregating at the level most appropriate for tracing resource costs and activity costs into other activities.
- Data import and export functionality, which minimizes reformatting.
- Visual aide and graphical user interfaces to simplify users' navigation through the ABC model and data.

Section 9–3 of Chapter 9 provides additional information about multidimensional reporting capabilities using on-line analytical processing (OLAP), which is becoming increasingly important to ABC software.

Today the cost department of the average business is looked upon as a right arm of first importance in management. Without the cost department today 90 percent of our businesses would be out of existence. . . . The cost department of the future is going to have more effect upon the business and upon the general management of business than any other single department. . . . And, gentlemen, in my opinion the major portion of the work of the cost department of the future is going to be applying recognized principles of cost analysis to sales expenses, for there is the greatest evil in present-day industry, the high cost, the extravagant, outrageous cost, of distribution.

James H. Rand. President, Remington Rand Company[2]

---

2. James H. Rand, "The Profit Element," *National Association of Cost Accountants (NACA) Bulletin,* vol. 9, no. 2, September 15, 1921.

CHAPTER 9

Sustaining the ABC/ABM System

It is a common criticism of cost accountants that they spend too much time in working out elaborate distributions of expenses which are unimportant in themselves and which do not permit of an accurate distribution. Undoubtedly some of that criticism is deserved, but it should also be remembered that once the basis for distribution has been worked out, it can generally continue in use for some time.

H. G. Crockett[1]

Many . . . have control and a knowledge of their business which meets their needs, and which they would be unwilling to surrender. On the other hand, many are sadly lacking in a knowledge of their own affairs . . . . Our [concern] is a problem for the present, and the business which is not equipped with the latest and best methods must have some immediate answer to its problem.

C. B. Williams[2]

9–1. STAND-ALONE VERSUS FULLY INTEGRATED ABC/ABM SYSTEM

In many organizations, a well-designed, periodically updated model is sufficient for their ABC/ABM needs. An off-line implementation enables them to substantially improve their managerial cost information without disrupting their day-to-day information system routines. Although it may be advisable to accumulate certain information under ABC/ABM that had previously been ignored, these data are used only for testing and updating the model, not for recording transactions. This scope is especially appropriate for small and mid-sized organizations, but it could also be an effective first step toward implementing ABC/ABM in a larger organization.

---

1. H. G. Crockett, "Some Problems in the Actual Installation of Cost Systems," *National Association of Cost Accountants (NACA) Bulletin,* vol. 1, no. 8, February 1921.
2. C. B Williams, "The Distribution of Overhead under Abnormal Conditions," *National Association of Cost Accountants (NACA) Yearbook,* 1921.

At the other end of the spectrum from the use of an off-line model is the full integration of ABC/ABM in the organization's day-to-day accounting and management systems. In these situations, ABC/ABM goes beyond the traditional role of cost accounting and becomes a primary source of information for improving business processes, forward planning, and eliminating or reducing non-value-adding activities. Under such a system, all production and reporting is adjusted to meet the requirements of the ABC/ABM system, as are the charts of account, cost center structures, inventory/cost of sales accounting procedures, interdepartmental charges, accounts payable and payroll cost distribution practices, financial and management reports, and every other cost-related facet of the accounting system. Obviously, major changes will also need to be made in the data processing system that supports the cost-accounting effort.

Revisit Figure 6–3. It described the spectrum or continuum spanning stand-alone systems from fully integrated ones. Figure 9–1 shows three dimensions that lead toward a permanent ABC/ABM production information system.

Figure 9–2 shows a diagram of a high-level, integrated ABC/ABM system.

9–2. UPDATING, REFRESHING, AND RERUNNING THE ABC/ABM SYSTEM

Companies that successfully complete their first ABC/ABM pilot will refine their activity dictionary and cost drivers. Then they will recompute their model. Rerunning the model is not always a pleasant experience. The approach, methods, and assumptions used in the initial pilot run may have been incompletely documented, which makes retracing those earlier steps difficult. But more agonizing, the preparation and reloading of all of the data can be an ominous task, particularly when the ABC/ABM work effort is in addition to the employees' regular jobs. Often the loading of the data comes from multiple, disconnected, and nonsimilar databases and different software languages. This further compounds the task. But these obstacles are surmountable through automation.

Concurrent with automating the systems integration, the pilot teams will ask teams from other companies, "How often do you rerun your model?" If it's justified, rerunning the model can potentially become a

FIGURE 9–1

ABC/ABM Integration

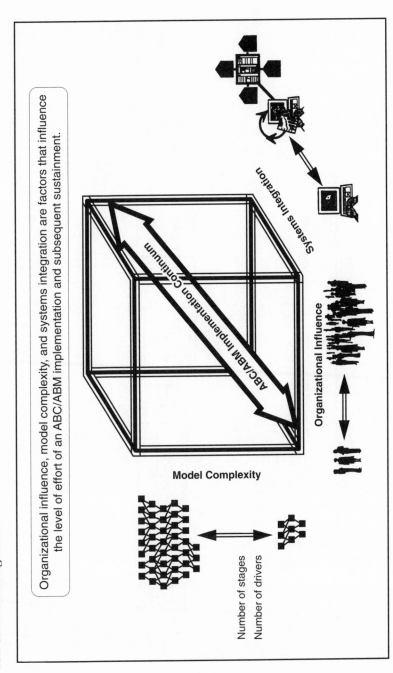

Organizational influence, model complexity, and systems integration are factors that influence the level of effort of an ABC/ABM implementation and subsequent sustainment.

FIGURE 9-2

ABC/ABM Production Systems

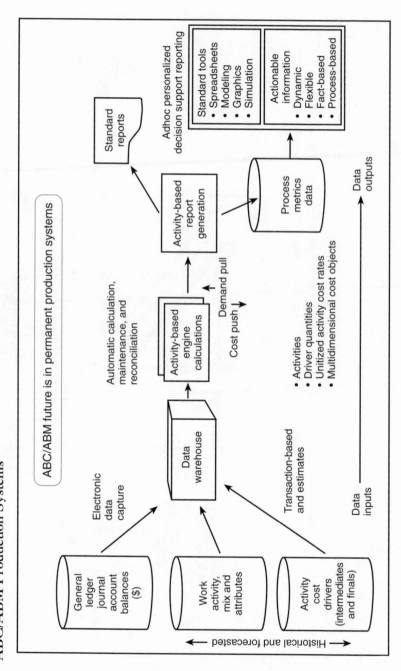

periodic event (e.g., monthly or quarterly). This means the pilot will eventually become a permanent production system. It will need to be manageable, reliable, and repeatable. (After all, isn't a "pilot" a demonstration for continuing use?) In many cases, companies update their models semiannually or at nonstandard intervals, recognizing that some of the data becomes stale with time.

In practice, all the data in the total model does not need to be entirely updated, even when the pilot graduates to become a permanent production system. An ABC/ABM model is constructed modularly. To an ABC purist, the model must fully equate the total resource general ledger spending amount to activity spending, and then equate that spending amount into the final cost objects. In addition, the cost assignment paths tracing the flow of costs from resources through activities and into cost objects must accurately capture both the diversity of the cost objects and the mix of how employees devote time to their work, all for the same time period.

But ABC/ABM principles include "closeness is better than precision" and 80/20 (Pareto's law) rule practices, which cannot afford ABC purist thinking. Since the flow of costs is initially constructed on cause-and-effect linkages for a time-slice of spending, consider what is necessary to recompute the next or successive time-slice. To the degree that events and behavior in the next time-slice (e.g., sales mix and employees' work content) are roughly repetitive and identical from the previous time-slice, some of the old data and relationships among resources, activities, and cost objects can be reused without needing revision. Some of the issues here are, How rapidly do data grow stale (i.e., change from the past)? How material is the error introduced into the next or successive time-slice of spending relative to reusing the prior time-slice data? Any error resulting from reusing the old data would be a consequence of deviations from the actual spending levels, activity mix, and cost object mix. For many businesses, these are likely to remain relatively constant on a month-to-month and quarterly basis. Updating the model is in truth a refreshing of the model for only the data that has significantly changed enough to have an impact to decision-makers.

Figure 9–3 reveals that only those data that are not constant between time-slices of spending, need to be replaced— all of the other data are reusable from the prior time-slice without degrading the computations. This ability to retain accuracy can immensely lighten the workload

FIGURE 9–3

Modular Approach to Refreshing and Updating Cost Data

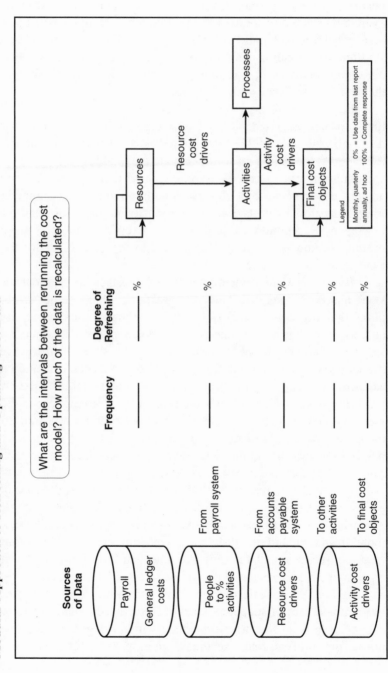

of refreshing the model. The insight here is that the model is in effect modular. The only parts of cost flow of the ABC/ABM model's network that need to be revised should meet these three tests:

1. The employee headcount or the mix of the employees' work activities should have significantly changed.

2. There is a substantial change in the distribution profile or mix of the cost objects consuming the activities. This includes additions and abandonment of products, services, or customers.

3. New activities are initiated or existing activities are eliminated.

In practice, companies will usually download their general ledger account spending balances using prebuilt automated linkages. This general ledger interface maintains credibility for those end-users who might otherwise discredit the model's results unless it reconciles with the general ledger expense balances. It feels good to them because it translates the profit-and-loss statements across functions. This downloading practice also automatically reflects any magnitude changes in headcount and purchase levels from the previous period's time-slice because the dollars show up in the payroll and expense account balances.

Significant time can be saved revising resource drivers. The percent mix in employee time-effort need only be reapportioned for those employees or groupings that have or are suspected to have changed sufficiently.

As permanent production ABC/ABM systems come to the marketplace, tools will be provided to automatically collect data in simple and noninvasive ways. For most data providers, they may electronically receive (via electronic mail or through their organization's communication network) an on-line input form. The only task for functional estimators is to enter their best, informed measures of how employees spent their time during a defined period. The data will then be electronically returned.

This technology solves any problems of poor or untimely responses. First, if responses are not reported by pre-agreed, scheduled due dates, the input form will be electronically forwarded to the nonrespondent's supervisor (that's always an incentive for an estimator to complete it). The form itself can provide the last-period or historical trend data to aid the estimator. The estimator may flexibly choose to pass the input forms downward to select employees for their direct input. The electronic input forms will always reflect prior revisions to the activity dictionary and changes in employee headcount levels. Finally, default data, based on reasonable assumptions, can be used if the estimator's data for unknown reasons is not transmitted by the deadline for the ABC/ABM system computation.

Similarly, activity cost driver data will be also directly transmitted from operational systems which accumulate the quantities of the activity cost driver transactions (e.g., number of invoices processed) along with the specific cost objects (e.g., invoice quantities by specific customer).

9–3. MULTIDIMENSIONAL ANALYSIS OF ABC/ABM DATA

One of the key goals of ABC/ABM is to give managers and employees insights into their economic structure and to stimulate them to ask deeper and richer questions about their organization's behavior. ABC/ABM data is more about findings than conclusions and subsequent actions. As organizations place greater emphasis on learning and discovery, managers and employees will be encouraged to explore more through unanswered questions than via standard reports that they did not define or design. Predetermined reports don't provide answers fast enough.

Most managers and employees are impatient when it comes to discovering and learning—they want answers immediately, not next reporting period. Fortunately for them, the uniting of ABC and multidimensional exploration software is now providing answers.

Multidimensional analysis allows for viewing the same costs across multiple hierarchies, such as by products, customers, distribution channels (e.g., direct, wholesaler), sales region, type of sale (e.g., promotion, special, standard), time periods, and so on. Multidimensional reporting allows end-users to slice, dice, rank, drill down, trend, pivot, sequence, and summarize data in organizational hierarchies; they can perform ad hoc calculations instantly. One of the most ideal applications of ABC data is cause-and-effect analysis of profit (or loss).

Multidimensional software turns days into minutes for employees accustomed to working with standard month-end reports. It allows them to interactively explore and analyze enterprisewide cost and cost-driver data. For the first time, managers can truly understand what is really driving the business.

Figure 9–4 shows a pyramid of software tools with the source data at the base. In the Information Age, employees will explore downward with executive information system (EIS) tools to analyze data that has

FIGURE 9–4

Multidimensional ABC

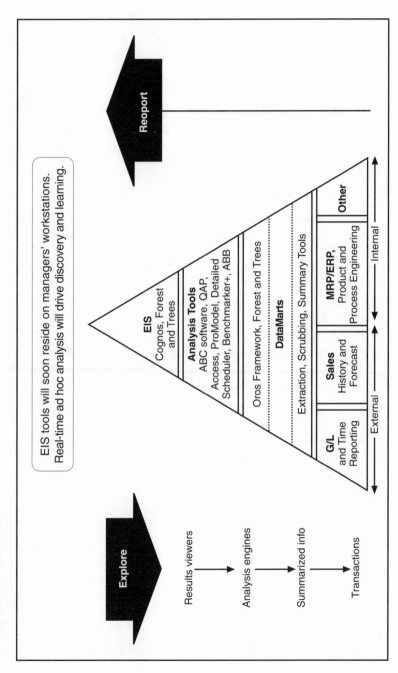

been extracted, relevantly calculated, and summarized for viewing. ABC/ABM is a tool, not a solution. The data brings visibility of symptoms of problems from which solutions can be inferred, researched, and implemented. On-line analytical processing (OLAP) tools are critical.

In the future, the finding of business solutions will shift away from full-time analysts to all managers and employees with computerized workstations or networked laptops. Instead of a few analysts spending all of their time analyzing and attempting to communicate conclusions, *all* managers will spend a portion of their time navigating and analyzing with multidimensional software. They will navigate intuitively with ABC data that fits their mental model on how activity costs flow and accumulate through process supply chains. Proficiency with OLAP will be common.

In sum, the objective is not to give managers and employees just data; it is to give them knowledge. Standard reports usually don't provide the answers; they lead to questions. Paper reports and computer monitors are two-dimensional mediums with limitations. Multidimensional analysis, particularly when combined with visualization graphics described in Section 7–11, will truly make workers smarter and increase the speed of business and commerce.

The top of the organization thinks, and the bottom acts. Too often, however, the bottom of the organization reacts. They react to unplanned events and out-of-tolerance business processes. The objective is to transform employees from somewhat helpless reactors into active participants who can intelligently create and shape their organization's future.

In sum, ABC/ABM pilots will become repeatable systems with credibility. Having these systems reporting in dollars, the language of business, will serve to operationalize process-based thinking.

The enormous expansion in computing capabilities has given today's designers of management accounting systems opportunities that could not have been dreamed about by their predecessors.

H. Thomas Johnson and Robert S. Kaplan[3]

---

3. H. Thomas Johnson and Robert S. Kaplan, *Relevance Lost: The Rise and Fall of Management Accounting.* (Boston, MA: Harvard Business School Press, 1987), p. 5.

CHAPTER 10

Final Thoughts on
ABC/ABM

Fortunately, the increased demands for excellent management accounting systems occur at a time when the costs for collecting, processing, analyzing, and reporting information have been decreasing by orders of magnitude.

H. Thomas Johnson and Robert S. Kaplan[1]

The activity-based accounting movement is embryonic. The transition for companies to ABC systems in the next 15 years is not a question of if but when. It is true that some companies tried ABC in the late 1980s or early 1990s and abandoned it. I believe we will look back on those failed experiments and dismiss them as inevitable false starts. ABC data is fundamental to the emerging styles of management, which are far more process-based and customer-focused than the traditional departmental or functional accounting approaches.

As stated repeatedly in this book, ABC is merely data that serves as a means to ends. ABC data should be considered as a way to achieve insights, both strategic and operational, into an organization's performance rather than as a replacement to the cost accounting system. Analysis with ABC/ABM data supports decision making and answers some great questions, as shown in Figure 10–1.

Today's traditional cost accounting gives managers and employees poor and frequently flawed visibility. As organizational focus increases on customers and the value-delivering processes that serve them, more managers and employees realize that they are poorly supported by departmental cost reporting and annual budgeting techniques. In this new age, you can't budget manage your way to cost management.

Activity-based information supports process-based thinking. ABC provides a framework for capturing costs that build up across business

---

1. H. Thomas Johnson and Robert S. Kaplan, *Relevance Lost: The Rise and Fall of Management Accounting* (Boston, MA: Howard Business School Press, 1987), p. 5.

215

FIGURE 10–1

ABC/ABM Answers Great Questions

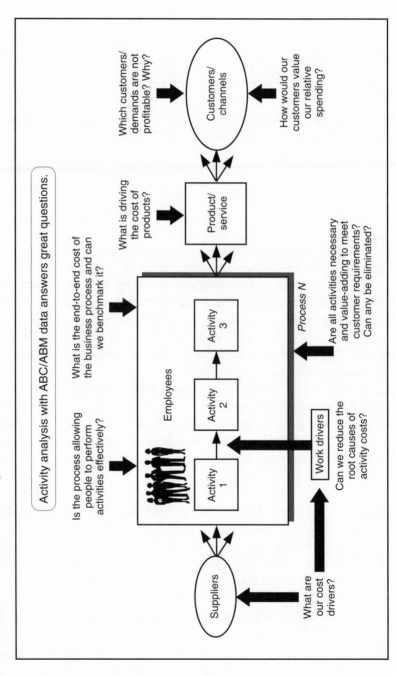

processes, which occurs in support-intensive and complex organizations. ABC properly associates costs with end-products and external customers and all the intermediate process outputs in between. This same data becomes the foundation for management of performance and implementation of process improvements (i.e., ABM).

What is the latest thinking regarding process improvements? The major message of the 1990s is that the rate of productivity increases exponentially with increases in targeted organizational scope and boundaries. On the basis of this discovery, organizations have scaled up continuous improvement projects into process reenginneering programs. Business processes are being radically redesigned around new views of customers, suppliers, and technologies; they are being restructured to leverage each organization's unique core competencies and to concentrate on truly profitable customers and geographies. And measurements of previously unexamined support and overhead functions have been included to achieve higher productivity increases. ABC/ABM data provide opportunities to get rid of the crabgrass between departments, and between trading partners.

There is now ample evidence in business periodicals and presentations at seminars and conferences that ABC has expanded well beyond manufacturing organizations and into service industries and government agencies. For example, as described in Section 3–5, the retail and food industries are launching collaborative supply chain initiatives called Efficient Consumer Response (ECR) or Quick Response (QR). ABC joins category management and electronic commerce (e.g., electronic data interchange, or EDI) to form the foundation for efficient and agile delivery of valued products and services to customers. And more frequently, trading partners in the supply chain talk about unbundled costs to serve and menu-pricing. (See Figure 10–2.)

In government, approaches such as performance-based budgeting and functional economic analysis (FEA) merely use dressed-up ABC data to support better decision making and deployment of limited resources. Furthermore, government-regulated organizations such as energy corporations or defense contractors are exploring commercialization or privatization; consequently, they must better understand their cost structures to be competitive.

Healthcare and financial institutions are also large service providers in world economies. Their interests in ABC make sense. They are in

FIGURE 10-2

Manufacturing versus Service Organizations

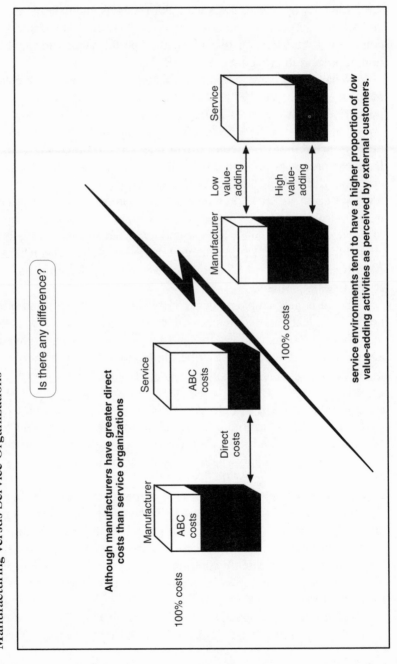

labor-intensive industries where work activities represent most of their costs. Thus, they need to know what their services actually cost and what activities create the most value relative to others.

The accountants recognize their role is changing. They face the choice of being leaders or followers. If they ignore process-based thinking, they'll wait for the 21st century *after* all organizations have transformed around virtual processes. But if they are leaders, ABC/ABM practices allow them to do it now—to help their managers visualize and manage business processes, plus get more accurate product and service costs as a bonus.

Regardless of the industry, every organization will eventually have to distinguish between cost cutting and cost management. There is a point at which an organization's senior managers don't want their junior managers and employees to solely focus on productivity and efficiency— they want everyone to achieve strategic plans. Obviously, a great way to make that possible is to give managers and employees the data and tools necessary to rapidly question, discover, and learn. The smarter organization wins the race—but there is no finish line.

Management accounting could not go forward were it not for the achievements that brought it this far. But, it must go forward. New times often call for new thinking.

John K. Shank and Vijay Govindarajan[2]

---

2. John K. Shank and Vijay Govindarajan, *Strategic Cost Management* (New York: The Free Press, 1993), p. 4.

INDEX

Other books of interest to you from Irwin Professional Publishing . . .

ABOUT THE AUTHOR

Gary M. Cokins, CPIM, is an internationally recognized expert, speaker, and author in advanced cost management and performance improvement systems. Following his receiving an industrial engineering degree with honors from Cornell University in 1971 and an MBA from Northwestern University's Kellogg Graduate School of Management, Gary began his career as a strategic planner with FMC Corporation developing business simulation models. With FMC's Link-Belt Division he served as Financial Controller and then Production Manager, which exposed Gary to the linkages between cost information, operations, performance measurements, and results.

In 1981 Gary began his management consulting career with Deloitte & Touche and KPMG Peat Marwick, initially implementing integrated business systems and ultimately focusing on cost management systems, including activity-based costing (ABC). More recently, Gary headed the National Cost Management Consulting Services for Electronic Data Systems (EDS).

Gary was the lead author of the acclaimed *An ABC Manager's Primer,* sponsored by the Institute of Management Accountants (IMA) and the Consortium for Advanced Manufacturers–International (CAM-I). In 1993 Gary received CAM-I's Robert A. Bonsack Award for Distinguished Contributions in Advanced Cost Management.

Gary is certified in production and inventory management (CPIM) by the American Production and Inventory Control Society (APICS) and is a certified implementor of theory of constraints (TOC). He serves on activity-based information committees including CAM-I, the Automotive Industry Action Group (AIAG), the National Center for Manufacturing Sciences (NCMS), the Agility Forum, Textile & Clothing/Corporation, the Society of Manufacturing Engineers (SME), Grocery Manufacturer's Association (GMA), and SEMATECH.

Gary's clients have included Philips Electronics, Sara Lee Corporation, TRW, Helene Curtis, The World Bank, the Federal Aviation Agency, Advanced Micro Devices, and Asea Brown Boveri.

e-mail: garyfarms@aol.com
phone: 810–642–0792
fax: 810–642–1789